# ACTION

An introduction to the
analysis of complex behaviour

# SYSTEMS

**David D. Clarke with Jill Crossland**

**METHUEN**

**London and New York**

First published in 1985 by
Methuen & Co. Ltd
11 New Fetter Lane, London EC4P 4EE

Published in the USA by
Methuen & Co.
in association with Methuen, Inc.
29 West 35th Street, New York,
NY 10001

Photoset by
Rowland Phototypesetting Ltd
Bury St Edmunds, Suffolk
and printed in Great Britain at the
University Press, Cambridge

*British Library*
*Cataloguing in Publication Data*
Clarke, David D.
Action systems: an introduction to the
analysis of complex behaviour.
1. Human behaviour
I. Title   II. Crossland, Jill
150     BF131

ISBN 0-416-36120-X
ISBN 0-416-36130-7 Pbk

*Library of Congress*
*Cataloging in Publication Data*
Clarke, David D.
Action systems.
Bibliography: p.
includes index.
1. Human behavior.   2. Animal behavior.
3. System theory.
I. Crossland, Jill.   II. Title.
BF57.C58   1985     300     85-13747

ISBN 0-416-36120-X
ISBN 0-416-36130-7

To Sara and Peter

# Contents

# Figures

# Acknowledgements

The authors would like to thank everyone who has been involved in the preparation of this book, especially Mrs Christine Allen who transcribed the lectures on which the book was originally based; the Universities of Oxford and Cambridge where the lectures were given; Mrs Ann McKendry who typed the many versions and revisions; Ms Mary Ann Kernan, Methuen's editor, who commissioned the book and supervised its production; and Dr Giovanni Carnibella who helped with the checking of manuscripts and preparation of reference lists.

The authors and publisher would like to thank the following for permission to reproduce copyright material:

W. H. Freeman and Company, Figures 7 and 8 from 'The evolution of behavior' by J. Maynard Smith. Copyright © September 1978 by Scientific American, Inc. All rights reserved; R. Harré, Figure 19; Tavistock Publications, Figures 21, 22, 23 and 25 from R. Harré (1976) 'The constructive role of models' in L. Collins (ed.) *The Use of Models in the Social Sciences*; Dr J. P. De Waele, Figures 26 and 27; Charles C. Thomas, Publisher, Springfield, Illinois, Figures 30 and 31 from S. J. Hutt and C. Hutt (1970) *Direct Observation and Measurement of Behavior*; Academic Press, Inc., Figure 32 from T. Winograd (1972) *Understanding Natural Language*, pp. 8–9;

# Preface

## The nature of action

There is a line in the constitution of Unesco which reads 'since wars begin in the minds of men, it is in the minds of men that the defences of peace must be constructed'.[1] In a way this is an unusual idea, because the problems of war and peace are typically considered in the rather impersonal terms of gross historical and political forces, which are seen as pushing human destiny before them like giant unstoppable mechanical bulldozers, not as originating in the thoughts and actions of individual people. Yet the difficulty in trying to understand such complex and disturbing courses of events as the processes leading to the outbreak of war is that they involve not only the psychological factors of suspicion, aggression and uncertainty, but also the properties of the social organizations and systems within which national boundaries are drawn up, and military measures devised to maintain or modify them. The problems are not to be understood in terms of actions alone, regardless of the systems of

[1] This is a verbatim quote and not my own choice of words. I agree wholeheartedly with the general sentiment, but I would not have chosen to use the word 'men', either as a generic term for people as a whole, or to suggest that women are unimportant in these matters.

meanings, laws and powers within which they are set; nor from the systems alone, without regard to the thoughts, decisions, feelings and actions by which they are energized. Clearly we *must* understand these matters, well and soon, if they are not to get out of control, and the only answer seems to lie in putting the two things together so as to study them as complete systems of action, not in using the piecemeal kinds of method which have been so common in the past.

On the whole this book deals with less dramatic and more commonplace kinds of examples, but here too the same point applies. There are many practical issues and problems in the world that stand to be solved only by reintegrating our understanding of individual and collective *action* with ideas from those disciplines in which complex networks of entities and processes are considered in their entirety, such as the *systems* sciences.

The book is about these two things, 'action' and 'systems'; with implications not just for human action but the action of other complex entities in the world too, like animals, crops, the weather or the economy, which form part of and impinge upon just about everything that we care about. Think of politics, medicine, the law, the way one brings up a family or pursues a career, how one makes a logical decision or comes to achieve a sense of self-understanding. These are all matters of human action, and it is our ability to understand and organize our part in them that is of real significance to us as individuals. We shall only become more adept at dealing with these aspects of our existence as we extend our awareness of the patterns and processes that make up such phenomena.

Much of psychology deals with the *behaviour* or *responses* of people and animals. Terms like *behavioural science* and *behaviourism* reflect the belief, held by many psychologists, that observable patterns of behaviour are the primary objects of study, and the only safeguard against a dangerous slide into loose theorizing and untestable speculations about unreal entities like 'the mind'. That might seem quite sensible at first, but the results have been viewed by many of us with increasing disappointment and disillusionment. Far from liberating us from an era of gullible introspection, and opening up a prospect of profound scientific enquiry, the influence of behavioural psychology has robbed the subject of much of the richness and relevance it promised to have, and has turned parts of it into a kind of parody science, where direct, firsthand experience of important life events is held to be worthless information. On the other hand, hastily contrived experiments, carried out under bizarrely artificial conditions, and much reinterpreted on their way to the printed page, are supposed to be worshipped as a kind of sacred truth. The typical reaction of students coming to psychology for the first time is one of dismay and disbelief that something that could be so interesting has been made to seem so sterile.

*Behaviour* also carries with it the connotations of a specific pattern of physical movements, objectively identifiable, and of limited duration. Sitting down is 'a behaviour'. Smiling and chewing food are 'behaviours'. A child who picks up or puts down a toy is 'emitting behaviours'. But much of what we do, and the terms we use to think about it ordinarily, are not like that. The important units of human activity, as named in everyday language, are different. They are more complicated, more abstract, longer drawn out, and less identifiable with particular physical movements. Moving house or resigning a job, adopting a child or committing a crime, are not really 'behaviours' in the technical sense, but they are certainly things people do, and for the most part more importantly and more interestingly than picking something up or putting it down. They are also more familiar and useful as everyday descriptive categories. We think of our lives and our decisions in terms like moving home or changing jobs, not in terms of limbs being extended and objects grasped. I call what I am doing at the moment 'writing a book', not 'grasping a fountain pen between the thumb and first two fingers of the right hand, and moving the nib over a sheet of lined A4 writing paper', and so on.

In this book, what we mean by *actions* are the real-life units and categories of 'things people do': the things that would figure in a diary, a novel, an obituary or a casual conversation about the day's events (although in a few cases the methodological points we make will be illustrated with behavioural examples).

## The nature of systems

The concept of 'systems' was born in biology, and has since spread outwards to influence most academic disciplines to a greater or lesser extent. The underlying doctrine of the systems approach is that structures and configurations of things should be considered as a whole, rather than merely examined piece by piece. In a highly complex system like the human mind or human body all the parts affect each other in an intricate way, and studying them individually often disrupts their usual interactions so much that an isolated unit may behave quite differently from the way it would behave in its normal context. Therefore, it is argued, it is more useful to consider the nature of the whole system at the same time. This perspective and the strategies of research it suggests have been applied to all kinds of systems, ranging from the very concrete (for instance, a piece of electronic circuitry) to the very abstract (like the system of mathematical equations which can be used as a model of the economy), and have had some currency already in the study of human action, although not as much as they should. The real difference between a piecemeal or atomistic approach, and a systemic or holistic one, is whether things are being taken apart to see what they are made of, or pieced together to see what they are part of. People tend to take the idea of the 'analysis' of action too literally, to mean decomposition of something into its component parts. The opposite, synthetic approach, sometimes called macro-reductionism, has something special to offer too. To face a practical decision or problem armed only with a piece-by-piece account of the action units involved is like trying to communicate in a foreign language armed only with a dictionary. All the pieces you might need to deal with are available and unproblematic individually. By far the greatest issue, though, is how they will interact, and how they can be managed, *in concert*. Jay Forrester, one of the leading exponents of systemic methods of policy making, has argued that the individual units and connections that make up a problem are often so straightforward and obvious that they need no individual study at all. Their properties can, in many cases, be assumed on the basis of general knowledge and common sense. The only place where special methods of investigation are called for is in the deduction of the overall properties and future behaviour of the system in which all these elements *interact*. We have no natural logic for inferring how complex systems will behave *even when we understand all their parts*, and it is here that complex computer simulations called systems-dynamics models can mimic the many interactions of the many parts, and show us how the system would behave as a whole, under the various conditions or policies we might create.

In spite of their considerable diversity, systems have certain common properties which make them appropriate for study as systems (and hard to study in other, more traditional ways).

1 *Systems are assemblies of parts connected together in an organized way.* The stones on a beach do not form a system; the cells in a brain do.

2 *The assembly is identified for a particular purpose.* This is an interesting property. What makes a particular collection of things a particular system is not an unchanging fact of nature, but a purposive decision by the people who study it. For one purpose, all the blood vessels of the body and their contents make up 'the circulatory system'. For a different purpose *the system* might be the respiratory apparatus, consisting of the lungs and their associated airways and blood vessels. Note that these are not mutually exclusive. Each of these systems contains parts in common with the other. What is part of the system and what is not depends on what we are studying on that occasion, and why.

3 *The parts are affected by being in the system and changed if they are taken out.* You cannot find out what someone's heart does by taking it out. In the first place, whatever it does, it stops doing it when you remove it. Secondly, what is left of the body does not go on obligingly displaying all its normal properties and capacities, excepting those for which the heart was specifically and solely responsible. What does happen, needless to say, is that an intact functioning system gets split into two parts, neither of which works without the other. All very obvious and rather silly, you may think, but what of a harder case? What if you study the members of a family as separate individuals, hoping to understand the family as a whole? Admittedly they do not cease to function completely, like a heart removed from the body, but they may not function *in the same way* outside the family, and the family may not be the same without them. If not, the study of each person in turn will not finally 'add up' again into the totality which was to be investigated.

4 *Systems typically do something.* They control a complex chemical plant, or co-ordinate public expenditure, or monitor the environment and take corrective action against unwanted change. This last one is an odd but fairly typical thing for systems to do, namely to stay the same in the face of influences which try to change them. The automatic pilot of an aircraft holds it on the same course, even though the wind may blow with varying speeds and directions. A thermostat keeps a house at the same temperature, even though

outside temperatures fluctuate considerably. This is called *homeo-stasis* or, literally, *staying the same.*

Furthermore, systems have boundaries, physical or conceptual lines of demarcation between what is inside them and what is outside. They may have no dealings with the outside, in which case they are *closed systems*; or they may exchange material, energy, information, and so on, in which case they are *open systems.* These often move towards and stay in states of equilibrium, where opposite forces and influences exactly cancel each other out. The central-heating system, for instance, keeps the house at a constant tempera-ture by supplying heat at just the rate at which it is being lost through the walls and roof. Open systems can not only maintain constant conditions, but can find their way to the same end result by a variety of means, and in spite of attempts to knock them off course. This is called the *equifinality principle.*

Different kinds of system can be *discrete* or *continuous.* They can change state in distinct steps, like the different displays of a set of traffic lights at a road junction, or else in smooth continuous progressions, like the changing pressures and flow rates in a network of pipes. They can also be *deterministic* or *probabilistic*, acting in a way that is exactly predictable from their circumstances (in prin-ciple), or else governed, at least in part, by chance factors. A pocket calculator is a deterministic system, if it is working properly; a gambling machine is a probabilistic one.

By putting together these two concepts, *action* and *system*, we arrive at the idea of 'action systems'. We have assumed that various human enterprises – careers, relationships, projects, strategies, con-flicts, and so on – are abstract systems of various kinds, and that, like other systems, they must be understood by mapping and interrelat-ing all the components and links that go to make them up. Of course there are many possible ways of trying to achieve this understanding. Some involve the use of mathematics or philosophical ideas; others make use of methods borrowed from the study of language patterns, or of computer programs which can then be used as active models. It is just this diversity of possible approaches that this book is trying to convey.

## Action systems

By now it should be clear from what has been said about action and about systems that a good many of the important aspects of human life really do take the form of action systems. Take as two key examples work projects and family relationships. They and their constituent events satisfy the criteria of actions. They are temporally extensive, salient and meaningful in everyday terms. They are also described in units with ordinary-language names, and grouped into equivalent instances having physically dissimilar manifestations, but with similar implications for more abstract levels of understanding. For instance, *disagreeing* is a common everyday action unit with a familiar name. But what is picked out by this term is a set of quite dissimilar sounds and movements, ranging from a shake of the head to a long verbal statement of opposition. Nevertheless the consequences for the subsequent course of events are usually the same, however the sense of disagreement is conveyed.

Projects and relationships also satisfy the criteria for being called systems. They consist of many parts, arranged in orderly, non-random ways. They are related to one another, particularly by temporal order, to form what are called *diachronic structures*, structures whose elements are arranged in the time dimension, and this is why *sequence analysis* plays a special part in their investigation, as we shall see later. The events take on very different implications if they are considered, or were to have occurred, in different contexts. Since it is only in relation to the context of other events that each can be understood, it is true to say that each element functions in relation to the rest of the system, and is changed by being removed from its context. As with the physical examples considered earlier, this is not just an interesting property of systems to think about, but also the chief practical reason for their requiring special methods of study. Orthodox experimental scientific approaches typically work on problems piece by piece, separating out each part, in order to find its true properties in isolation from the confusing influence of other factors. That is fine where it is appropriate, but in the study of systems, by and large, it is not.

Our examples are singled out as systems for particular purposes. Projects are usually studied so as to plan, monitor, improve and complete them. Relationships are identified as part of enjoying and participating in them, but also to study, repair, predict, choose and make practical provision for them.

Lastly, projects and relationships, like other action systems, *do* something. Or, more precisely, their underlying control systems, their 'generative processes', do something, of which the project or relationship itself is the historical progression and/or end result.

There is another sense in which the ideas of *action* and *systems* belong together. We have already remarked upon the peculiar state of certain branches of psychology at present, and their tendency to leave new adherents disappointed that they should be so different from, and so irrelevant to, what we think of as psychology in everyday life. Clearly something is missing from the subject, as presently conceived. What is not so clear is exactly what needs to be done to remedy the deficit.

Two things in particular seem to be needed, and they are somewhat like the moves we are suggesting towards actions as units of analysis, and more systemic methods of study, respectively. The first requirement is that at least *some* branches of psychology should be built upon the foundations of ordinary commonsense experience. This is not because commonsense experience is necessarily all that rich, accurate and comprehensive, or because the standard criticisms levelled against its subjectivity, unreliability and cultural specificity are all that wrong. The reason we must take it more seriously is that for most people, and for most purposes, most of the time, it is *all there is*. For the lay person, commonsense knowledge represents the state of the art in psychological reasoning and problem solving, so by far the most useful thing that professional teachers and researchers in psychology could seek to do would be to enrich and extend it. Instead, they are more often determined to ignore it at first, and subsequently to replace it with something quite separate and independent. This places the lay person in a dilemma. Our 'scientific' psychology adds nothing to theirs. The two are irreconcilable because ours, the 'official' psychology, was never designed for such a reconciliation. The lay person's psychology is far too important, not to mention interesting and credible, to be abandoned. Faced with no other practical alternative, most people reject scientific psychology as being largely irrelevant to them – *and rightly so*. This will be the downfall of academic psychology, unless something is done soon to remedy it.

It may seem that this talk of building on commonsense knowledge is all rather unscientific. *Real* science, however, is very largely built on commonsense foundations, at least in its early stages. Later on the commonsense basis may be modified and superseded perhaps, but only because it is part of, and can be carried along by, the stream of scientific progress. If our predecessors' commonsense physics and biology had been left out of their scientific account of the natural world, not only would academic physics and biology have floundered about for want of a provisional framework to start from, but the commonsense conception of these things would have fossilized by virtue of its complete disengagement from the tide of scientific developments. This is just what is befalling 'scientific' psychology.

The remedy, though, is not to study and codify commonsense knowledge. That is the opposite mistake, also common in psychology. Most of psychology ignores commonsense knowledge and the remainder studies it. Both are wrong. We need to extend it. What we should be studying are those things that are outside but contiguous with commonsense psychology. In short we should be treating it as part of the literature. Like the literature it should be taken as provisionally true for the time being, but subject to revision in particular cases, when shown to be suspect. It should not be trusted uncritically, or totally ignored, or discounted out of hand, or regarded as irrelevant. New research should be counted as novel only if it extends the combined sum of scientific and commonsense knowledge. However, at present, research is often held to extend scientific knowledge even when it is only putting into the official literature for the first time what was previously obvious but un-documented common knowledge. Similarly, new research should be regarded as adequately linked to its precedents only if its presenta-tion relates it to the relevant items of previous research *and* common-sense experience, *and not otherwise*. The study of action, by attend-ing to ordinary meanings of events and ordinary units of analysis, but then looking for unfamiliar links and processes behind them, goes some way towards realizing this objective.

The other desirable modification that psychology and its related disciplines need to make is to get away from the minutiae, and the decontextualized analysis of isolated events and measures. Quite apart from their self-evident triviality, the minutiae which are so often researched have another, more obscure reason for meriting less attention than they receive.

Human activity is hierarchically structured. Configurations of small units make up larger units, which make up larger units still. When I have written enough words I shall have a sentence. A good collection of these will make up a chapter, and a few of those will constitute a book. At first sight this seems rather like saying that enough baryons (protons and neutrons) and leptons (especially electrons) will form an atom. A reasonable assortment of atoms will make a molecule. Pile these up neatly and you could have a crystal, and so on. But there is a crucial difference. The natural particles arrange themselves. They embody the processes of their own deployment, and it is from the most *fundamental* particles that the larger collections take their properties. The fundamental particles determine the properties of the atoms, which determine the properties of the molecules. The causal hierarchy is driven from the bottom upwards, and so its explanation lies in moving *downwards*, retracing the process to the origin of the higher-order properties. Here the minutiae are crucial: they are the *fundamentals* of the whole system.

But words (and actions) are not like that. *They* do not arrange themselves according to intrinsic properties and processes. Nor do the fine units determine the gross ones. I am choosing my words to suit my sentences, not the reverse. In action and in language the hierarchy is driven from the top down, not from the bottom up. It is the gross plans and actions that are fundamental, and *that* is where *fundamental* research should be directed, not at the matters of fine detail. Those are secondary, and stand to be explained *by* the gross patterns, not to provide the explanations *of* them. You buy a certain ticket and pack a certain coat *because* you are flying to New York, not the reverse. The whole determines the parts. The fundamentals of this hierarchy are at the top.

In fact the real situation is rather more complicated still. There are really two hierarchies at work. The hierarchy of action units is the *product*, and it is a *constitutive* hierarchy, a structure of parts and wholes. What goes on inside the head of the actor is the underlying generative *process*, which organizes and controls the pattern of actions. This is a *regulative* hierarchy, a multi-unit control system in which higher-order units are not made up of lower-order units, but rather receive information from them and send instructions to them.

The more correct account of the top-down organization of the action hierarchy is to say that small units of action are regulated by low-level controllers in the regulative hierarchy, which are governed by high-level units, which give rise to and are reflected in the gross or higher-level structures of the action hierarchy. So it is only *as if* the gross structure of behaviour controlled the matters of fine detail. The basis of all this is a consideration of the *overall* picture. Everything else proceeds from that. For this reason too, a systemic, overall method of analysis is of special importance. Both of these points are served in the synthesis we are calling *action systems*.

In bringing together the research traditions of *action theory* on the one hand and *systems theory* on the other, the difficulty does not lie in reconciling the two. They are strikingly compatible. The difficulty is in bringing either of them (let alone both together) into the mainstream of the behavioural sciences, where, on the whole, methods have to be rather more atomistic and positivistic than these, in order to be acceptable. Orthodox researchers in psychology often claim that their main concern is to be scientific, and that *our* methods are *un*scientific. However, we have no quarrel with their objective. We too think it is important to be scientific, but we see that as involving a theoretically rich and methodologically complex and diverse range of ideas and procedures, as typified by the advanced sciences. To confine the arena of legitimate enquiry to a narrowly conceived area of experimentation and measurement is not to be scientific but to be *scientistic*, to make a fetish of the trappings of science as they appear in the simpleminded stereotype of the nineteenth-century physics laboratory, and that is not such a good thing. The present fashion for regarding biological aspects of psychology as scientific, and the more abstract aspects as 'mere social enquiry', for all political and financial purposes, is both a consequence and an endorsement of this fallacy.

## The structure of the book

If a transformation of psychology is to be brought about, a good deal of new research along rather unorthodox lines will be needed. In the meantime we have tried to describe the existing styles and traditions of research from various disciplines which can already start to serve this purpose. We have begun close to home with methods that are used in conjunction with mainstream experimental research. Quantitative, statistical, even experimental methods, although often used in the ways we are arguing against, can also serve more holistic and more humanistic purposes. These applications will be dealt with in Chapter 1. In Chapter 2 the unorthodoxy – many would say the heresy – begins in earnest. Much of the dissatisfaction of the last ten years with standard conceptions of social psychology has been articulated and prompted by the works of Rom Harré, an Oxford philosopher of science, who believes that social psychology would have to change very radically in order to draw on the real precedents of the advanced sciences. His programme of research, called ethogenics, the study of 'meaning-giving' processes, is described in Chapter 2.

In the arguments above we have already likened the structure of action to the structure of language. This theme, sometimes called structuralism, will be explored in Chapter 3. In Chapter 4 we return explicitly to the idea of systems models and methods for the analysis of action, with a discussion of computer simulation and artificial intelligence, mathematical modelling and cybernetics. In these disciplines the systems concept has been developed beyond a general philosophy, and formulated into specific and powerful research tools. Here we shall be able to give the clearest and most explicit account of the coming together of action and systems.

Apart from the common theme of 'action systems' running through the four chapters, we have not attempted to give them any particular unity. The primary purpose of this book is to demonstrate the variety and diversity of the approaches that exist, and the broad range of disciplines in which they are to be found.

There are suggestions for further reading at the end of every chapter. Each list is quite long and ranges from popular paperbacks for the general reader through to the technical articles which researchers would need to consult in order to start incorporating these methods into their own work. We have not attempted to mark out which references are of which kind. It is nearly always self-evident from the type and title of the publication. Clearly books from popular publishers of paperback series for general readers are at one end of this continuum, and technical articles with jargon-laden titles in obscure scholarly journals are at the other, by and large.

Many of the ideas and research methods described in the book were devised for different purposes and within different conceptual frameworks from the one into which we have grafted them. In some cases their authors would not have had action or systems explicitly in mind, and for this reason they do not all come across in exactly the same way, or in the terminology we have outlined here. For the most part we have tried to present each idea in its own terms, but without completely obscuring the relevance of the theme of action systems. In the last chapter it returns to the forefront of the argument.

## How to use this book

Throughout the book we shall examine the methods available for these different types of analysis of action systems, showing in simple terms, with the use of diagrams and examples, the sort of 'tool-kit' which is now available for their study. We have collected different methods from various disciplines, and for this reason many of the people who read this book will already know at least one of the approaches treated here in some detail. For psychologists, Chapter 1 will be very familiar, while philosophers will already know the contents of Chapter 2, linguists will know Chapter 3 and computer scientists Chapter 4. However, despite the fact that many readers will find that parts of the book give only a simple description of their own area of expertise, we hope that each specialist will find something of interest in the less familiar material covered in the remaining chapters. For the general reader we hope there are new and interesting ideas throughout the four chapters.

There is no single best way to read this book. Starting at the beginning and reading to the end has its merits, but there are other alternatives too. People who are specialists in one or more of the fields covered might do well to skip over the familiar material, if they are reading through in order. Since each chapter, and each subtitled section within the chapters, is reasonably self-contained, the browser who likes to take sections out of sequence should not be at much of a disadvantage. No particular checking back to earlier sections should be necessary. We have used a number of examples to make the methodological points clearer and more interesting. However, we have resisted the temptation to make every point through examples, since that would create the false impression that these methods are tied to very specific applications. To take an analogy, if basic arithmetic were *always* taught with a particular example of, say, vegetables being added to and taken from a basket, it might be harder to see the universality of the procedures, and delay the realization that the same operations have just as much part to play in the modelling of an economy, the designing of bridges or the prediction of planetary motion. In much the same way, we see many of the techniques described here as contributing to a 'calculus' of action, with applications ranging from psychiatry to market research, and from strategic analysis to artificial intelligence. The power and importance of these procedures lies in their *separability* from the specific domains for which they were first devised, and in which they are most commonly found, and their application to apparently unrelated issues. For this reason we have chosen to put some of the points in their more general and abstract form, so that the overall spirit of the book will not be unduly obscured by the peculiarities of the examples we use.

In addition to the four types of research described in the four chapters, and the four clusters of disciplines on which they are based, there are also four problems about action systems which the chapters attempt to deal with in turn. In Chapter 1 it is the problem of multivariate description: how large numbers of measures of each of a large number of things can be reduced to a useful summary picture. In Chapter 2 it is the issue of meaning, and its role in the understanding of conduct, together with, or instead of, cause and effect. In Chapter 3 the problem is that of the serial order of events, and how in particular whole families of sequences, such as the set of all possible sentences in a language, can be captured in a single unified description. In Chapter 4 the problems concern the prediction and management of events. This is the point of the whole exercise. Understanding action systems is not just a pleasant pastime; it is a practical necessity. Action systems can wreck economies and start wars, or they can draw people together and create understanding and achievement. How they are managed is crucial. In the last chapter of the book we shall start to consider how understanding leads to improvement. If we know how these systems work, we can make them work better, by creating sophisticated models on which policies can be tried and their pitfalls detected, before we make the real action systems themselves the proving ground for our mistakes.

Oxford, November 1984                        DAVID CLARKE

# 1

# Experimental and related methods

This chapter deals with some ideas and methods which arise in *experimental* research. The usual purpose of an experiment is to examine the relationship between causes and effects in the world by manipulating the supposed cause and observing the supposed effect. For instance, in attribution experiments, different groups of subjects are typically given different kinds of information about a hypothetical event, in order to see how it affects the explanations they arrive at for the event in question. The given information is the *cause* or 'independent variable', and the resulting conclusion is the *effect* or 'dependent variable'.

We have assumed that you are familiar with the basics of experimental design, procedure, statistics, and so on. Hopefully what is laid out in the following pages will provide some supplementary information to add to the fundamentals of experimental knowledge you already have. If this is not the case, you might like to look at a reference book on experimental design, such as Carlsmith, Ellsworth and Aronson (1976) or Stahl and Hennes (1980).

The unifying theme of the first section, and throughout the book as a whole, is one of synthesis: how scientists can take complex and diverse information and create a coherent framework within which to interpret it. The corollary of this is that many problems remaining at the moment in the analysis of human action persist only because of the prevalence of the opposite perspective – a misplaced desire to collect and analyse data in a piecemeal fashion. Usually in psychology the object of investigation is treated as a structured whole to be reduced to its component parts. We propose the opposite but complementary approach: that the object as it is first encountered be seen as part of something larger, which leads us to ask questions like 'What is it a part of?', 'What other components are also part of that larger whole?', 'In what way do they combine?', and so on. This approach leads to a very different style of explanation – explanation by reference to higher rather than lower levels of description. This may seem to be a simple anti-reductionist philosophy, but it is not completely so, because we are still dealing with the same objects and the same sort of relations between levels of description as the reductionists, except that we are examining them from lower to higher levels of description instead of the reverse. We are not against a broadly mechanistic style of explanation based on the idea that entities and events often take their properties from, and are hence to be explained by reference to, the subcomponents of which they are made, provided that the superordinate systems of which they are part are considered as well. This can be especially relevant for the understanding of action systems, where events are typically influenced as much by their context as by their constitution.

This chapter will illustrate some of the ways in which quantitative measures – whether subjective in origin, like someone's rating of a commercial product on an attitude scale; or objective, like a measure of pulse transit time in a hypertensive patient – can be combined mathematically to give a relatively comprehensive picture of a complex phenomenon, showing each part in the relation it has to the whole. Despite the stereotype which many people hold, quantitative science is not exclusively concerned with the reduction of complicated processes to a few simple units which can be understood in isolation from each other.

## Problems with experiments

Before exploring the rather more unorthodox forms of behavioural analysis, we shall consider a fairly basic, hypothetical experiment concerning the effect of age and diet on weight. Two important concepts should be explained at the outset. One is what we call *given-instance analysis*, and the other is the idea of *non-surrogate investigation*. To elaborate on the first: a given-instance analysis means, literally, that the instance under examination has been specified and cannot be changed, as with a biography, an outbreak scenario for a conflict, or a particular pattern of events over time. In each of these cases one is free to gather different kinds of data, but the *content* of investigation is decided in advance. If the task were to make sense of a particular life story, it might be possible to interview the person, study diaries, observe, interview acquaintances, and so on, but it would not be legitimate to study someone else instead, merely because *their* life story was more accessible. The instance on which research is to be done is not freely variable. Likewise, substitution of different material such as an artificial laboratory analogue is not possible, which is what is meant by the second feature of this kind of design, namely the use of non-surrogate material. Imagine you are in the role of a chemist who has been given an unknown substance and told to find out its composition. You would not throw it away and replace it with some other substance from the laboratory to analyse as a substitute. Experimental methods will often work only with surrogates, or with artificial cases created in the laboratory – which is why for applied research problems it is important to develop non-surrogate methods. This is one of the things we shall try to deal with in the course of this book.

To return to our fairly orthodox example, we can use an experiment to examine cause and effect, taking for granted for the time being that one can establish a cause-and-effect relationship by manipulating what is taken to be the cause and observing what is taken to be the effect, and looking for some pattern of systematic or concomitant variation between the two. We shall also assume, for the time being, that finding the previously unknown causes of known effects is the essence of scientific explanation. In Chapter 2, however, we shall need to re-examine that idea more critically to consider alternative forms of explanation. These will involve the 'powers', or capacities, by virtue of which people and things have the behavioural repertoires they do, and in the case of *human* systems we shall need to consider the explanation of events by reference to the meanings of those events for the people involved.

Figure 1 shows how we might see the results of an investigation into the effect of age and diet on people's weight as they grow older. Running along the base of the graph (the 'abscissa') is the first

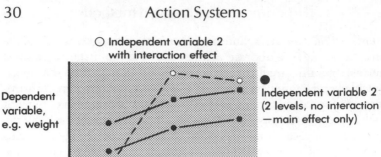

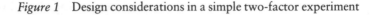

*Figure 1* Design considerations in a simple two-factor experiment

independent variable, age, with the 'levels of the variable', which are 10, 20 and 30 years. The vertical axis (the 'ordinate') of the graph displays the dependent variable, weight. You can see a rapid weight gain between the ages of 10 and 20, and a less rapid weight gain between 20 and 30. The second independent variable, diet, is represented in the diagram as the difference between the bottom and top undashed curves on the graph. The bottom curve shows the relationship between age and weight for somebody on a low-calorie diet, and the top curve for somebody on a relatively high-calorie diet. Although, as you can see, people get heavier as they get older, and different diets result in different weights, it is important to note that the addition of the second independent variable, a different diet, has not altered the pattern of relationship between weight and age. The curves are identical in form, and it is only their position that differs. However, if you turn to the dashed line you will see a different kind of outcome, called an 'interaction effect', in which one variable (diet) alters the relationship between the other variables (age and weight). The former case is known as a 'statistical main effect', where one quantity affects another but does not alter a pattern of relationships. The latter case is called a 'statistical interaction', where changes in the level of one variable influence the pattern of relationship between other variables.

It is the implications of this interaction effect which will be central to some of the problems and methods explored in the following chapters. Very often the discovery of interaction effects in an experiment is welcomed as an interesting, though complex, aspect of the findings. There is a danger, however, that intensely interactive phenomena will produce interactions not only within experiments, but between the experimental variables and the unconsidered factors. In that case the pattern of experimental findings will be peculiar to the conditions prevailing at the time, and will be hard to replicate. It might be argued that large numbers of interactions in an experiment are not a reason for rejoicing at all, but a sign that a more systemic and less piecemeal mode of investigation is called for.

Rom Harré, who coined the term 'ethogenics' for a novel approach to the study of action in which the central issue is the way it is rendered meaningful, has put forward a simple criticism of some kinds of experiment, of which even the simplest designs can fall foul. The 'two-by-two' design in Figure 2 contains two causal variables, each with two levels, and one dependent variable. Suppose high and low anxiety are the two levels of the first independent variable, and sex (male or female) are the levels of the second. The dependent variable may be test scores on some performance measure. Harré suggests that a design of this kind is intrinsically misleading, because the second independent variable is not a variable at all but a 'parameter', a fixed defining property of the type of people involved. In other words gender, unlike anxiety, is not an attribute of a person that can be varied as part of the experimental procedure, and yet in spite of this, anxiety and sex are treated as having comparable roles in the experiment. The level of anxiety *can* be considered as a genuine variable because it may vary over time for a single individual. A group of moderately calm subjects could be introduced to the experiment, and half of them could be made to feel anxious, while the other half could be reassured in some way to decrease their level of anxiety. In this way the variable might be manipulated to produce high and low levels in two otherwise identical groups of subjects. Of

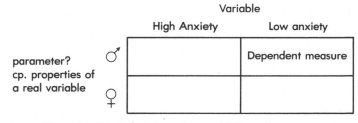

*Figure 2*   2 × 2 design mixing variables and parameters

course, this kind of experimental treatment would not be viable for gender. One would not start with a group of sexual neuters and inject one half with male hormones and the others with female hormones! What one has in this case is a 'package deal' consisting of some subjects who have been male all their lives and others who have always been female. Even if we think we are investigating the nature of their biological or cultural sexuality, it is inevitably confounded with other factors that accompany their sexual status and identity, which the experiment does nothing to isolate, as it would with a genuinely controlled variable.

Harré suggests that using a mixture of variables and parameters violates the basic logic underlying experimentation, and so leads to results of rather dubious validity. The point of a properly designed experiment is to show that certain effects vary with, and only with, their candidate causes. In a weak experiment, such as the one described above, there are many possible causes varying together, and so it is not clear which of them the effect is responding to. Furthermore, since many of the vital social properties of people are based on their individual and (relatively) unchanging parameters, this problem is always likely to beset the application of standard experimental methods to the analysis of everyday human behaviour. Many of the standard formats of investigation used in the behavioural sciences suffer from problems of the kinds we have discussed very briefly, so we shall be drawing many of our examples from the less orthodox types of study which can be found in the literature.

Having given a basic introduction to certain aspects of experimental reasoning and the problems raised by statistical interaction, we can now move on to something a little more substantial and possibly less familiar. There are a number of quantitative tools which have been developed in a variety of disciplines to simplify and capture the essence of complex data. The next section is a description of some of the organizing frameworks used to synthesize data from different sources, including case studies, field observation, laboratory experiments, and so on. The first of these frameworks is called 'game theory'.

## Action as games

Game theory started off as an applied-mathematical and operations-research tool at about the time of the Second World War, and has since migrated into the field of descriptive and explanatory social science. (Operations research is the application of scientific problem-solving methods to real-world problems, such as the optimal time interval at which to replace something which is prone to failure with age, but expensive to replace.) Game theory has had a curious history, having evolved from behavioural technology to behavioural science, which is the opposite of what one would expect, and perhaps it is this reverse transition that has led to some of the misunderstandings of the theory. Initially used as a tool to prescribe rational choice, under conditions of uncertainty about the effects of each choice, it has subsequently been suggested as a possible descriptive theory of how people behave in the natural course of events. This seems to be contradictory. It has only been successful as a decision-making procedure because people do *not* behave *spontaneously* in the way it suggests. If game theory had been a good description of spontaneous behaviour, then following it as a deliberate procedure would have led to the same outcomes as not deliberately following it, and it would have failed as a helpful technique.

The problem which game theory tries to solve is this: if people have to take a decision under conditions of uncertainty, if they are trying to control a social, economic, military or governmental system in which the things they do influence what happens, but do not absolutely determine what happens, they end up in a dilemma. They are faced with a variety of possible actions, and whichever they choose to execute it could produce diverse effects on the world they are dealing with. If they were in competition with another individual, then choosing any one of the given options would produce changes in the situation which could in turn rebound on the actor. Likewise the opponent would be faced with the same sort of choice. Between them the outcome would be determined, although individually neither one of them would be in a position fully to decide the outcome, because that would depend on the combination of their joint actions. It is therefore easy to see how the situation could produce a logical spiral, with each party trying to outguess the other; each considering the response their actions might elicit; and each trying to account for the possibility of their opponent switching to a different style of reasoning. One way of breaking free from this spiral of confusion is to represent the overall situation in the form of a 'pay-off' matrix.

Figure 3 shows a stylized pay-off matrix for two people A and B, each with two possible courses of action, called 1 and 2. A's options

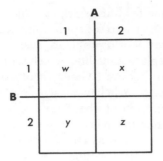

*Figure 3*   Stylized pay-off matrix

are represented by the two columns in the matrix, and B's by the two rows. For every combination of something that A or B might do, there is a pay-off in the corresponding cell of the matrix (that is, a numerical representation of the relative benefits or losses resulting from that combination of actions). Optimal decisions about the course of action to be taken by each actor can be calculated by analysing the distribution of pay-offs in the matrix. In this case there is only one pay-off shown for each cell, implying that whatever A wins B loses, or vice versa. Since the sum of their gains and losses would therefore come to zero, this particular kind of game is called a 'zero-sum game'. If the pay-offs for the two sides are different, if A's wins or losses are not the exact opposite of B's, then it is called a 'non-zero-sum game'. The non-zero-sum game is conventionally represented as in Figure 4, with each cell in the matrix being split to show two different values, one for each actor. In this example the choice of action 1 by A, and 2 by B, leads to pay-offs of $x$ and $y$ to A and B respectively.

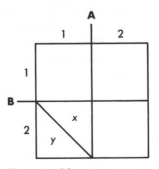

*Figure 4*   Non-zero-sum game

How can this notation be used to study other patterns of action? One well-known example is the 'Prisoners' Dilemma' game, which illustrates the dilemma of trust, and its influence on people's willingness to adopt a particular role or strategy. The underlying principles of this game can be generalized to all sorts of situations. It has recently been used by students of international relations to make mathematical models of the problems involved in international disarmament talks, with investigators casting the various negotiating positions in the format of a matrix game, to establish what might be the best strategy for the two sides to adopt.

**Prisoner A**

| | | Not confess | Confess |
|---|---|---|---|
| **Prisoner B** | Not confess | 1 year only | 10 years for B<br>3 months for A |
| | Confess | 3 months for B<br>10 years for A | 8 years each |

*Figure 5*     The Prisoners' Dilemma game

In the 'Prisoners' Dilemma' you are asked to imagine two prisoners kept in separate cells, with no means of communicating with one another. The police are trying to get a confession from each of them, by explaining that the potential penalty for their crime will be increased if one confesses and the other does not. The prisoners, unable to reach an agreement between themselves, have to rely purely on their trust, or lack of trust, of each other. The sort of penalties they face are as follows: if neither of them confesses they get off relatively lightly with a one-year sentence each, because of the doubt that would surround their guilt. If they both break down and confess, their guilt is established, but they would receive some measure of leniency and get a penalty of eight years' imprisonment each. However, the real problem arises when one confesses and the other does not. If, for instance, A confesses and B does not, A stands to be imprisoned for only three months, because of his co-operation with the police, but B would get ten years, because his guilt and his lack of co-operation have been established beyond doubt. (Obviously the story is not realistic, but it serves as a mnemonic for the structure of the dilemma, which is common to a whole class of real situations, as shown abstractly in Figure 6.) Each person has to try to act in a way that will be of most benefit to himself, so what choice should be made?

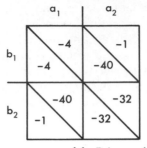

*Figure 6*   Abstract structure of the Prisoners' Dilemma game

Consider the plight of B. As far as he is concerned he has two options – to confess or not to confess. Neither choice seems particularly advantageous, because if he does not confess he could be imprisoned for either one or ten years, depending on A. If he does confess, he could get three months or eight years, again depending on A. If B is in a trusting frame of mind, he might assume that A would not confess, and so by keeping silent he could leave their guilt in question, and they would both stand to get off with only one year. But here they run into the dilemma of trust. If B holds his ground and A *does* break down and confess, then B's situation would become much worse. So can he afford not to confess? Gradually the game gravitates to the state of affairs where they both confess and receive a sentence of eight years. But, had it been possible for them to trust one another enough, they could both have got a sentence of only one year. Therein lies the prisoners' dilemma. It is complicated to describe but easy to see in the matrix. One of the main advantages of such a game-theory formulation is the ease with which it can represent (if not always resolve) just what the essential dilemma is, in a complex and seemingly intractable situation.

Keeping the Prisoners' Dilemma game in mind, we shall now try to apply the same kind of reasoning to a more realistic situation. In the study of animal behaviour it is something of a puzzle why animals fighting for survival, or arguably for the survival of their genes, often seem to restrain their aggression. Surprisingly, a fight to the death is relatively rare. There seems to be some sort of mechanism which inhibits the use of all-out conflict in the animal world. But what genetic advantage is gained by the animal that moderates its fighting, when everything seems to be at stake? A way of answering this question is suggested by Maynard Smith's Hawk–Dove game.

Assume that two animals meeting in a situation of possible conflict can either flee, or stay and fight. If an animal chooses to flee it would neither gain nor lose anything in evolutionary terms, so for the purpose of the game we will give this option a pay-off of zero. However, if the animals fight one another, there could be one of three consequences. One of them may sustain serious injury. This is a high price to pay and can be given a negative pay-off of −20. Or one of the animals could be victorious and gain access to territory, mates, and so on. This would be an advantage and can be assigned a pay-off of +10. Finally, it is possible that the fight may be evenly matched and become long drawn out, exhausting both animals and gaining them nothing. This possibility can be assigned a pay-off of −6. We have now represented the four possible outcomes of a conflict, according to the evolutionary advantage or disadvantage they confer. The key to the allocation of these scores is the assumption that the animals stand to lose more when they are seriously injured than they stand to gain in any single victory. Every important property of the game will follow, regardless of the exact pay-off values used, as long as this assumption is met.

What then is likely to happen during individual encounters, given that there are two possible strategies: the 'Hawk strategy', which involves all-out fighting until the individual is either victorious or badly injured, and the 'Dove strategy', which means fighting, but retreating when at a serious disadvantage? We have to consider what would happen to the prevalence of animals using these two strategies in a population that was in constant interaction. Would the Hawk strategy gradually predominate and destroy the Dove? Could the Dove dominate and eliminate the Hawk? Would the overall advantage come from some mixture of strategies?

Consider the four logical classes of encounter that could take place within the Hawk/Dove population as shown in Figure 7. In the case of Hawk meeting Hawk the overall pay-off would be −5, calculated by using a simple equation (shown in the top right of the figure). The first equation shows that each Hawk stands to win half the time (pay-off ½ (+10)) and also stands to lose half the time (pay-off ½ (−20)), giving an overall expected pay-off for Hawk–Hawk encounters of −5. This would be like the average score or 'batting average'

**Hawk / Dove**

| | | |
|---|---|---|
| Serious injury | $-20$ | $E(H,H) = \frac{1}{2}(10) + \frac{1}{2}(-20) = -5$ |
| Victory | $+10$ | $E(H,D) = +10$ |
| | | $E(D,H) = 0$ |
| Long contest | $-6$ | $E(D,D) = \frac{1}{2}(10) + \frac{1}{2}(-6) = +2$ |

|  | | H | D |
|---|---|---|---|
| Pay-off shown for this individual | H | $-5$ | $+10$ |
| | D | $0$ | $+2$ |

ESS = Hawk $\frac{8}{13}$

Dove $\frac{5}{13}$

*Figure 7*    The Hawk–Dove game (from Maynard Smith 1978)

over a long series of such encounters with assorted outcomes. As it is the *expected* pay-off for a *Hawk* that meets a *Hawk*, it is shown as E(H,H). Likewise the average pay-off for a Hawk meeting a Dove would be +10, because the Dove would retreat from the conflict every time, and the Hawk would always be victorious. From the Dove's point of view it would lose nothing when encountering a Hawk, because it would flee. Two Doves fighting could either win or become involved in a long, unsuccessful fight. The net pay-off for this encounter is therefore +2.

(Of course this is a non-zero-sum game, but the convention of showing both pay-offs in a split cell has been simplified in this case to show just the pay-offs to the animal whose strategies mark the rows of the matrix. The game is symmetrical and the same considerations apply to the other animal too.)

Is there a strategy which is evolutionarily stable, that is to say immune to infiltration by some variation? If in such a case an individual in the Hawk/Dove population changed its strategy, it would be disadvantaged, and the population would return to its former stable strategy. In a population consisting only of Doves the average pay-off from their encounters, as we have seen above, would be +2. If an individual now adopted the Hawk strategy it would have an evolutionary advantage initially, gaining +10 every time it fought one of the Doves for territory, or for mates. It would gain a definite advantage over the pure Dove colony. Over time, the advantages of the Hawk strategy would lead to the number of Hawks increasing, but only up to a point. A pure Hawk colony would not be optimal either, nor free from the possibility that the Dove strategy would be to the advantage of its practitioners, up to a point. It may seem surprising but the Dove strategy would also be an advantage in a Hawk colony. On most encounters the Dove would meet a Hawk and lose nothing, but a Hawk in a similar situation would stand to lose five points on average in the predominantly Hawk–Hawk encounters. Once again the Dove strategy would be at a selective advantage, with its users breeding profusely, and the incidence of Dove strategists increasing with the growing number of offspring. Whether it started with more Doves or more Hawks, there would be an in-between position, a mixed strategy, towards which the population would tend over time. The point of equilibrium (based on these simple representations of the possibilities) would be to use the Hawk strategy $8/13$ of the time and the Dove strategy $5/13$ of the time. This is called the 'evolutionarily stable strategy' (ESS). Any departures from this strategy would be disadvantageous, and would therefore tend to be self-cancelling.

By extending the Hawk–Dove idea we can examine a more complex situation called the Hawk–Dove–Bourgeois game. The Hawk and Dove behaviour options stay as before, but the inclusion of the 'Bourgeois' strategy adds an interesting twist to the game. The Bourgeois player resolutely defends its own territory by adopting the Hawk strategy towards intruders. However, if the Bourgeois strays on to another animal's territory, or meets another animal outside the confines of its own territory, it then adopts the Dove strategy. The inclusion of Bourgeois behaviour alters the overall dynamics of the game. There is now a single or 'pure' strategy which is evolutionarily stable (bottom right-hand cell, Figure 8). This means that the Bourgeois population is immune to infiltration by use of the other behavioural options. In a pure Bourgeois population, the use of the Hawk strategy results in a number of occasions when the Hawk meets a Bourgeois, and in this situation the Hawk's average pay-off is only 2.5, as opposed to the pay-off of 5 which would have been achieved using the Bourgeois strategy. Conversely, use of the Dove strategy would reduce the pay-off for that individual from 5 to 1. In this way, it is possible to show that the Bourgeois strategy is the evolutionarily stable one, that is, the state towards which the system

**Hawk / Dove / Bourgeois**

$E(H, B) \rightarrow \frac{1}{2}E(H, H) + \frac{1}{2}(H, D) = -\frac{5}{2} + \frac{10}{2} = 2.5$

$E(D, B) \rightarrow \frac{1}{2}E(D, H) + \frac{1}{2}(D, D) = 0 + \frac{2}{2} = 1$

likewise for E(B, H), E(B, D), E(B, B)

|   | H | D | B |
|---|---|---|---|
| H | −5 | +10 | +2.5 |
| D | 0 | +2 | +1 |
| B | −2.5 | +6 | +5 |

ESS = pure strategy 'bourgeois'

*Figure 8*    The Hawk–Dove–Bourgeois game (from Maynard-Smith 1978)

will gravitate, and which will resist significant change, by allowing the practitioners of that strategy the best chance of passing it on to the next generation.

To recapitulate: one of the main problems with the analysis of social behaviour is the uncertainty under which each individual chooses his or her own behaviour, when unsure of the reaction of the other(s), and hence of the benefits or drawbacks of the choice. The formulation provided by game theory captures these uncertainties and their implications, and enables us to calculate which behavioural strategies would be expected to emerge and persist on the grounds of their unimprovable (evolutionary) advantage. This is not to go back on the earlier point that game theory is a good decision-making aid in so far as it is a bad descriptive theory of behaviour. In the last two examples, game theory was being used in a different way, as a calculus for inferring the behavioural consequences of an evolutionary theory of behaviour, not as a behavioural theory in its own right. This is an important distinction to get right. To draw an analogy with the natural sciences again, Isaac Newton's use of differential calculus (or 'fluctions', to use his term) in the analysis of planetary motion was not in itself a theoretical statement about the reasons for the planetary orbits being as they were. *That* lay with his laws of motion, and the regularities of gravitational attraction. Calculus was the mathematical tool by which the empirical implications of the theory could be worked out, so as to check them against observations. Whatever the theory had been, the same form of calculus would have been appropriate for the deduction of its consequences. So too, in this case, game theory is useful for calculating the implications of a variety of psychological conjectures, even when the underlying control process to be discovered is nothing like the deliberate reasoning through of a game-theory problem, as a way of choosing the course of action to take next.

## Following sequences

Now let us move on to some rather different forms of behavioural analysis, starting with the analysis of behaviour sequences. In its simplest form, sequence analysis is a way of examining sequences of events unfolding over time, ranging in principle from the parts of speech in a sentence to the various stages in an individual's biography, or the major events of an epoch of history.

The stream of action is first divided into discrete events, which then have to be classified into groups of functionally similar items. These might be the stages or moves leading up to the outbreak of a conflict, for example. Often letters or numbers are used as the 'names' for these groups or types of events. The criterion of classification is all important: elements of behaviour must be put in the same category only if they would fit appropriately in each other's context. This is the guarantee that they are treated similarly by whatever principles of sequencing are at work. It would be no use classifying verbal threats and other kinds of threatening behaviour as instances of the same class of event if they had dissimilar consequences. The upshot would be that this 'single class' of event would show variable and unpredictable properties in all subsequent analyses, whereas the two different types of event, had they been properly distinguished, would each have had its own clear implications.

The next stage is to draw up what is called a transitional-probability matrix. The coded events are considered in pairs: for instance, if event types X, Y and Z occurred in a sequence in that order (using arbitrary letters to stand for the categories of events), there would be two transitions between events to be counted – namely, XY and YZ. They would be added to the tally of events in the cells of the matrix where row X meets column Y, and where row

Y meets column Z, respectively; they would then be divided by the total number of transitions, to give the probability of that particular transition being observed on any occasion. In the study of 'outbreak scenarios' for armed conflicts, X, Y and Z might be respectively the delivery of ultimata, failure to comply, and the outbreak of hostilities. The YZ cell of the transitional-probability matrix would show the probability of fighting breaking out after an ultimatum had been ignored, and likewise for every other pair of events or 'transition' which could occur. By continuing in this way for all the transitions between all classified events in the data, one can build up the complete transitional-probability matrix for the sequence in question.

There are many ways of continuing the analysis of such a summary table, but the essential step is to test for the statistical interdependence of the rows and columns – which is to say the dependence of subsequent events on preceding events. If the prior and subsequent events are independent, then their probability of occurring together will be the product of their respective probabilities of occurring in any context. That would appear in the matrix as a set of observations falling in any cell with a probability equalling the product of their probabilities of falling somewhere in the same row and somewhere in the same column. Significant departures from that expectation indicate that the events are interdependent. Since the row and column represent the first and second event of each pair, this in turn implies

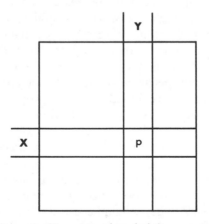

*Figure 9*   Transitional-probability matrix

that the earlier event *does* influence the later one, and that over all the sequence has a genuine *sequential* structure which would not be found in a randomly ordered collection of events. Note that it is not enough just to show that some transitions in the matrix are more probable than others, because even by coincidence it would be expected that some pairs of events would occur more frequently than others, because some individual events are more common than others. The strength of this method is that it detects the transitions which are remarkably common or uncommon in relation to the *different* rates at which each transition would be expected to occur by chance. In our example it would be important to know, not just the general likelihood of conflict in a given interval of time, but whether particular diplomatic moves beforehand have the effect of making it more or less likely than it would have been otherwise.

As we have given only a brief and simple introduction here to the basic method of sequence analysis, we shall return to this in Chapter 3, in relation to language and the language-like structure of other kinds of behaviour.

## Simplifying complexity

The next type of analytic tool we shall look at is multivariate statistical analysis. This is a type of statistical procedure designed to draw together, in the form of a 'numerical précis', large batteries of figures or measures. Often the result is presented in visual form, making it easier to give a summary statement of the data before working on further statistical analysis. Starting with factor analysis, we shall describe the rationale behind a family of statistical techniques which have been increasingly used in the analysis of spontaneous action patterns, to categorize the constituent actions and to detect consistencies over time.

If we have a number of things to be measured – in this case let us suppose people – and a number of different measures of each one on a number of different tests, we generate another matrix, another box of numbers, where for every person there is a column, and for every test a row, and where for each individual's score on any given test there is an entry in the corresponding cell. We now have to consider how these data can be reduced to a manageable summary form, which can be used as the basis for a map of the possible dimensions

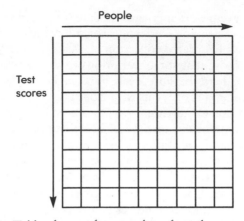

*Figure 10*    Table of scores for a number of people on a number of tests

and types of variation in what was measured, whether in the general case it was people, situations, buildings or whatever. Is it true that all the test scores gathered from each individual subject necessarily measure different things? It may be that, to a greater or lesser extent, we are measuring the same things over and over again under different names and with different procedures. It may be for instance that there are fewer separate types or dimensions of intelligence than there are different intelligence tests. If so, how can we find out how many genuinely different facets of the world we are *really* measuring, what they are, and which tests measure each of them? The underlying dimensions of variation which emerge when this type of analysis is used are called factors, and they give their name to the technique which is known as 'factor analysis'.

It may be that two of the original tests used were measuring the same thing, in which case one is largely redundant. If this were true, or even partly true, the entries in their respective rows would be highly correlated. If two tests, for instance I and J, were measures of much the same property of people, we should expect someone scoring highly on I to score highly on J, and vice versa. Similarly, for every pair of tests, the coefficient of correlation between them indicates the degree of redundancy. Using these correlation values between every possible pair of tests, a new matrix can be drawn up which does not show people on one axis and tests on the other as before, but instead gives the correlation between each pair of tests.

Such a matrix only needs to show one triangular portion, because,

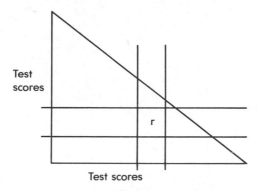

*Figure 11*   Lower-half diagonal (correlation) matrix

if test I is correlated with test J, then J is equally correlated with I, so the complete square matrix would have shown the same values twice over, in the top right and bottom left corners. By convention, the bottom left corner is usually shown alone and is known as a 'lower-half diagonal matrix' or 'lower-half triangular matrix', and it is the common form of representation for symmetrical data.

But what exactly do we mean when we say that two measures like I and J are correlated? How can this be visualized in such a way that whole arrays of correlations can be represented, giving a picture of the different components and dimensions of variation that arise in the original data, emphasizing *independent* dimensions of variation, and omitting what is redundant? There is a way in which the process can be pictured quite simply. Starting with an individual person's scores on tests I and J, we can imagine them plotted on a two-dimensional graph. There would be a point in that two-dimensional space for each person, corresponding to his or her score on I, plotted against his or her score on J. If this were done for everybody who had been measured originally, we would have a picture of all the pairs of scores on tests I and J for the sample. A 'swarm' of points (known as a scattergram) would be created in this plane, and the shape of that swarm would reflect the nature of the relationship between the tests which is described by the correlation coefficient, an index of the mutual predictability of the two measures.

If the variables were perfectly correlated, then all the points would lie along a straight line, and any person's score on one measure would be exactly predictable from a knowledge of the other – which is to say that one or other measure would be *completely* redundant.

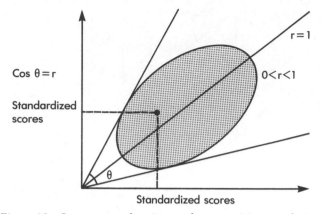

*Figure 12*    Scattergram showing moderate positive correlation

In reality, perfect positive correlations are hard to come by, so in most instances there will be a positive (or negative), but not perfect, correlation. Generally the points will form an ellipse roughly following the direction of a straight line (called a regression line) showing the ideal plot of one variable against the other. The degree of correlation between the two variables can now be thought of as the thinness or fatness of the ellipse on either side of the regression line. The more highly correlated the variables are, the thinner the swarm of points and the more exactly it is confined to the ideal regression line itself. (Very similar arguments apply to pairs of variables which are negatively correlated, which again means that they are predictably interrelated, but as one gets bigger the other gets *smaller*. On the scattergram this would show up as an elliptical swarm or streak of points running from top left to bottom right, whereas the scattergram for a positive correlation is stretched out from bottom left to top right.)

As we have seen, narrow elongated swarms correspond to high correlations, and round fat swarms to low correlations. If the variables have been expressed in standard and comparable units, by stating each value as the number of standard deviations by which it falls above or below the mean for that variable, the scattergram will have a further interesting property. The fatness or thinness of the swarm can now be described by the angle its tangents make at the origin or bottom left-hand corner of the graph, and the cosine of this angle will behave exactly like the correlation coefficient. (The cosine of an angle describes the proportions of a triangle containing that angle and a right angle. More specifically it is the ratio of lengths of the two sides subtending the angle in question.) When the variables are perfectly and positively related, the swarm will be a single line passing through the origin, its two 'tangents' will have an angle of zero degrees between them, and the cosine of that angle will be 1.0, as will the correlation coefficient. If the two variables are *unrelated*, then the scattergram will be spread throughout the plane, its tangents will make an angle of 90 degrees at the origin, and so the cosine of this angle will now be zero, like the correlation coefficient. In a similar way, as the swarm becomes drawn out in the other direction and the correlation coefficient becomes negative, the angle subtained by its tangents will become increasingly obtuse and will have a negative cosine, still corresponding to the correlation coefficient. (Incidentally, this is why variables which are uncorrelated, or which describe quite independent kinds of variation between which there is neither influence nor predictability, are often often called 'orthogonal', meaning at right angles.)

Within this framework the two tangents can be thought of as standing for the two variables, while the angle between them stands for the correlation between the two variables. The two lines are called 'test vectors'. (A 'vector' just means a variable which has the properties of both magnitude and direction, like the velocity of the wind, as opposed to something that has a magnitude but no direction, like the temperature of the air, which is called a 'scalar'.)

Now let us go on to consider three variables at a time. Imagine that three vectors were to be positioned so as to represent the interrelationships between three tests which we will call I, J and K. From our initial measurements we would have established the correlation between every possible pair of the tests (that is, the angle between every pair of vectors). From these pairwise values for the angles we would then have to construct the correct overall configuration of vectors, and describe the kind of space in which that configuration could occur. To take a simple case, suppose the correlation between the first two vectors, I and J, was described by an angle of 30 degrees, and the correlation between J and K was also equivalent to an angle of 30 degrees. If it transpired that the correlation between I and K was 60 degrees, then clearly they could all be arranged in a single flat plane (see Figure 13). In this particular case the pattern of correlations for the three tests would only need a two-dimensional space

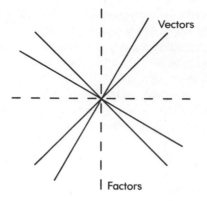

*Figure 13*    Four test vectors described by two orthogonal factors

in which to build up the picture, which is the same as saying that there are only two independent dimensions or sources of variation in the three original measures.

Of course, in practice, factor analysis would not be used with such easily visualized material. Normally there would be something like twenty or thirty different test vectors, which could at worst involve us in constructing a twenty- or thirty-dimensional map, with all the dimensions at right angles! This is hard to imagine but mathematically is a straightforward extension of the ideas and calculations one would use in going from the 1 to 2 to 3 orthogonal dimensions we are more familiar with. The saving grace of all this is that correlations mean redundancy, and redundancy means that the picture can be simplified without loss of information. In just the same way that three vectors turned out to be describable using only two dimensions in the above example (depending on just what the correlations were between the vectors), even twenty or thirty vectors, if they were adequately correlated, could be described quite accurately in a space having only a handful of dimensions. This is precisely the purpose and the net result of doing a factor analysis. Although the number of newly created dimensions in the space (called the *factors*) may be rather more than three, and therefore hard to picture all at once, it is still much easier to think in terms of a map with, say, five or six dimensions, than to try to grapple with twenty-eight.

Before moving away from factor analysis, it may be helpful to review briefly the logic that leads to its use as a tool not only for looking at the correlational relationship between measures, but also for showing up the dimensions of the space in which these measures lie, which in a sense is the overall structure of the 'system' being measured.

Let us go back to the example where three test vectors could be fitted into a two-dimensional space. The relationship between the three vectors is given by the data and cannot be changed. But the two orthogonal dimensions within which that relationship is described are an arbitrary invention, so it does not matter which two axes we use, provided they are at right angles and in that same plane. This can be compared with the way that features on a physical map are indexed by the grid-reference lines. The relative positions and distances between points cannot be changed to suit the map makers' convenience, but the reference grid is relatively arbitrary and could be rotated relative to the map without the geographical facts of the map being distorted in any way. If there were some reason for locating the features of the British Isles on a grid of lines running from north-east to south-west, and from north-west to south-east, instead of from north to south and east to west, that system would work just as well (as long as it was used consistently), and our beliefs about the size and layout of the country would be quite unaffected. It is just the same with factor analysis. The factors work like grid-reference lines and can be rotated in any direction that suits us, provided the positions of the test vectors *in relation to each other* (which is like the basic geographical arrangement being mapped) are not changed as well. So, provided we keep the vectors in the same pattern in relation to one another, we can rotate the factors in various directions while analysing their changing relationship with the vectors. This is what is called 'factor rotation'. Just as the correlations between tests could be described as angles, the angles between the features of this newly created map can be described as correlations. In other words, the angles between the factors and the test vectors that completely characterize the final picture can be translated back to the language of correlation coefficients. It is as these correlations between the factors and the original tests (which are called the 'factor loadings' of the tests) that the results of a factor analysis are stated. In effect, a new set of synthetic 'measures' of the original people or objects have now been created, and their correlations with all the original tests established. They are uncorrelated with one another and therefore summarize the most information in the least number of dimensions.

The purpose of factor rotation, together with the criteria by which it is done, involves the alignment of the factors as far as possible with the main 'bundles' of adjacent (that is highly intercorrelated) test vectors, so that each factor is easy to interpret as the counterpart of a set of tests which are uniquely associated with it. The associated tests provide a way of measuring the factor in practice, since in itself it is only a hypothetical scale with no concrete measurement procedure. In Figure 13 there are four test vectors running diagonally in the plane of the diagram, and two factors describing them, running vertically and horizontally. The problem is that each factor describes all four vectors, and each vector needs to be described in terms of both factors. If the two factors could be rotated by about 45 degrees, each factor would then coincide closely with one pair of vectors, or, to put it another way, the information in each pair of vectors would be summarized by a single factor.

Sometimes, to achieve the appropriate correspondence of factors and vectors, the factors have to be rotated in relation to one another, so that they are no longer at right angles. This is called 'oblique rotation'.

Of course, it would be possible to have as many factors, and therefore dimensions, as vectors. Some criterion is needed to simplify the picture, accommodating the information with the best compromise between parsimony and accuracy. One way of doing this is to look at the amount of variance accounted for by each of the factors (which are always numbered and printed out by the computer in

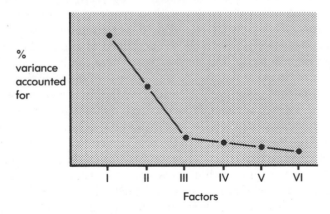

*Figure 14*    Variance accounted for by successive factors

decreasing order of the amount of variance accounted for) in the form of a graph. This often shows a rapidly falling portion of the variance being accounted for by the first several factors, and then a 'dog-leg' after which the remaining factors account for a small and slowly decreasing proportion of the total variance. The latter factors can often be ignored, leaving an economical and sensible number of dimensions. If things have gone well, it should be possible to translate the original test scores for the people who were measured into the corresponding 'factor scores', showing where each individual would appear in the new system of dimensions represented by the factors. In Figure 15 you can see an example of just such an outcome. 'Granny's' factor scores have been used to locate her on the factors neuroticism and extroversion. You will notice that neuroticism is a unipolar factor (it runs from zero to very neurotic and *not* from very 'un-neurotic' to very neurotic). However, extroversion is a bipolar factor, and runs from very extrovert to the opposite, which is very introvert. Now we have a clear picture of 'Granny' as plotted on the two factors introversion and neuroticism, as well as a conception of these as major 'axes' of variation in human character. Because these are the dimensions contained implicitly in the original tests, this space in which people are now being located is called a 'test space'. If we had carried out the whole procedure the other way around from the outset (which would often be quite sensible, although not in this particular example) and had chosen to intercorrelate person with person across all tests, instead of test with test across all the people, we could have produced tests (represented by points) plotted in a person space. To do that we should need more tests than people, whereas to locate people in a test space we needed more people than tests.

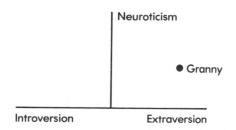

*Figure 15*    Person plotted in a test space according to factor scores

Very often the elements would be the salient people in the subject's life, but they could equally well be commercial products, political parties, holiday resorts, or anything for which the person has a conceptual map. Next, a group of three elements is selected, and the subject is asked to say which is the odd one out and why. If the subject picked out one of three people, and said it was because that person was unkind, then the concept 'unkind' would become the first strand of the subject's system of differentiation to be elicited, and would be written against the first row of the grid. This procedure is repeated with different groups of three elements, to elicit a whole list of such concepts with which to label all the remaining rows of the table. These concepts are called the 'constructs'. The subject can now rate all of the elements on all of the constructs, showing to what extent each property is found in each person. In this way the table can be filled out with ratings running from, say, 1 to 7. Any cell containing the number 7 indicates that the construct on that row is very highly applicable to the element on that column, and so on through all the values down to 1, which would be used when the construct is highly *in*applicable. We are now in a position from which factor analysis can begin, having a table of many things (the elements) measured on many variables (in this case, subjective variables called the constructs). Now, just as before, the factor-analysis procedure can be carried through to the point where the person's elements are seen as points plotted in a construct space.

In this account the term 'factor analysis' is being used in a loose sense to refer to a family of statistical methods which includes principle-components analysis and factor analysis (as used in a second and more specific sense). This may seem confusing, but it is a common trick of language to use the same term generically and specifically.

A common and very flexible way of collecting information to use in a factor analysis is the 'repertory-grid technique', which emerged from Kelly's theory of 'personal constructs'. The purpose of this is to map an aspect of the world as seen through the eyes of a subject, and to plot things which are salient for him or her in terms of the dimensions and spaces which summarize his or her own conceptual scheme. There are many variations on this technique, but to avoid confusion only the most basic form will be described here. First of all a blank table (the grid) is drawn up, and the subject nominates a list of salient items (which are called the elements). These are then written across the top of the table, labelling the different columns.

Next, we shall look at some similarities and differences in procedure and usage between factor analysis and a related method called 'cluster analysis'. It starts from the now familiar similarity matrix, which tells us how similar each of a number of things is to each of the others. However, in this case we start from the similarities between the things being measured and not the similarities between the measures being used. A way of summarizing these data, and of conceiving of them as part of an overall structure, is to think of each of the things that have been measured as a point in a 'dissimilarity space'. This means an arrangement of things such that, the more dissimilar they are, the further apart they are positioned in that space. When all the items have been located according to that criterion, the data should appear as little islands – 'clusters' of points, sprinkled about in the space.

In order to summarize the relationships between these clusters, we must construct a kind of family-tree diagram or 'dendrogram', showing the closest items (and therefore the most similar) spanned by a little bridge low down in the diagram, and the less similar items spanned by bridges higher up. There are different variations on this technique, depending on the criterion used to measure the distance

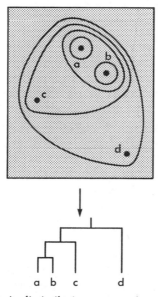

*Figure 16*    Points in dissimilarity space and associated dendrogram

between one cluster and another. It is easy to define the distance between any two points, but the distance between two clusters is more complex. Should the farthest or nearest members of the clusters be taken as the points to measure from? The choice could make all the difference to the picture of the clusters and their component items which is built up. The simplest procedure is a technique called 'single-linkage cluster analysis', where the distance between any two clusters is taken to be the distance between their nearest members.

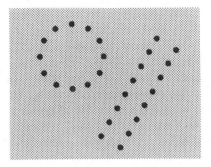

*Figure 17*   Chains and cline in dissimilarity space

On a cautionary note, if you *do* make the wrong choice of distance criterion, some funny things could happen. If the points in the dissimilarity space happened to be arranged either as two parallel rows or as a circle (known as a cline), as shown in Figure 17, it would be easy to end up with a misleading result. Each of the parallel lines would be shown as a separate cluster, implying that all of the points in the same line are similar to one another, and the two lines are dissimilar, which is really not the case. Likewise in the case of the cline, the items might end up looking like a tightly knit cluster, while the considerable distance (dissimilarity) between items on opposite sides of the circle was left unrepresented. However, despite these complications, cluster analysis is another very useful means of pulling together strands of measurement and producing a visual-summary diagram. One of its uses is as a stage in the procedure of sequence analysis mentioned earlier. After the stream of events has been divided into separate, discrete units, or 'parsed', and before the sequence analysis proper is carried out, it is necessary to classify the events into recurring types or families, according to their relations of commutability or 'mutual swapability'. If a measure of mutual swapability for each pair of potential event types is calculated, such as the correlation between them in the frequencies with which they precede and follow the same things, this measure can then be used like a similarity measure in a cluster analysis. As a result, any groups or clusters of similar events will be found to show up as a condensed group of points in the dissimilarity space, or as a bundle of closely interlinked 'twigs' in the tree diagram. This would indicate that they are *combinatorially* equivalent, and can then be regarded as instances of the same type of event in further sequence analyses.

In another related procedure called multidimensional scaling, the starting-point is as for cluster analysis, and the end result rather like a factor analysis. Starting with the dissimilarities of a number of items, each item is represented as a point in a space, in such a way that the distance between every pair of points is proportional to the dissimilarity between the pair of objects they represent. This may require a hyper-space (a space having more than three orthogonal dimensions), just as factor analysis often does. Like a factor analysis, this reveals the number of independent dimensions of variation that were latent in the original measures, the position of the measured items in relation to these summary dimensions, and the nature of the real-world measures and differences that each dimension represents.


To summarize, the point of this chapter has been to show how a variety of quantitative measures, from subjective ratings to objective quantities, can be combined using statistical and other mathematical techniques to form relatively comprehensive and synthetic pictures of complex phenomena, as opposed to the kind of analysis which many people associate with quantitative science, in which the picture is steadily reduced to fewer and simpler elements. In the subsequent parts of this book we shall turn from quantitative to other conceptual methods for doing this, at the same time moving further towards the idea of 'action systems' as the complex, interwoven, dynamic configurations in which human experiences, decisions and activities generally occur.

## Further reading

Argyle, M. (1983) *The Psychology of Interpersonal Behaviour*. 4th edn. Harmondsworth: Penguin.

Avedon, E. M., and Sutton-Smith, B. (1971) *The Study of Games*. New York: Wiley.

Bannister, D., and Fransella, F. (1971) *Enquiring Man*. Harmondsworth: Penguin.

Barnes-Gutteridge, W. (1974) *Psychology*. London: Hamlyn.

Berkowitz, L. (ed.) (1964–) *Advances in Experimental Social Psychology*. New York: Academic Press.

Berkowitz, L. (1979) *A Survey of Social Psychology*. 2nd edn. New York: Holt, Rinehart & Winston.

Broadbent, D. E. (1973) *In Defence of Empirical Psychology*. London: Methuen.

Brown, H., and Stevens, R. (1975) *Social Behaviour and Experience*. Open University. London: Hodder & Stoughton.

Capella, J. N. (1980) 'Structural equation modelling: an introduction'. In P. R. Monge and J. N. Capella (eds), *Multivariate Techniques in Human Communications Research*. New York: Academic Press.

Carlsmith, J. M., Ellsworth, P. C., and Aronson, E. (1976) *Methods of Research in Social Psychology*. Reading, Mass.: Addison-Wesley.

Child, D. (1970) *The Essentials of Factor Analysis*. London: Holt, Rinehart & Winston.

Clarke, D. D. (1983) *Language and Action: A Structural Model of Behaviour*. Oxford: Pergamon.

Cohen, D. (1977) *Psychologists on Psychology*. London: Routledge & Kegan Paul.

Coleman, A. (1982) *Game Theory and Experimental Games*. Oxford: Pergamon.

Dawes, R. (1980) 'Social dilemmas'. *Annual Review of Psychology*, 31, 169–93.

Elms, A. C. (1975) 'The crisis of confidence in social psychology'. *American Psychologist*, 30, 967–76.

Ginsberg, G. (ed.) (1979) *Emerging Strategies in Social Psychological Research*. Chichester and New York: Wiley.

Gottman, J. M. (1979) *Marital Interaction*. New York: Academic Press.

Gottman, J. M. (1981) *Time Series Analysis*. London: Cambridge University Press.

Guilford, J. P. (1965) *Fundamental Statistics in Psychology and Education*. 4th edn. New York: McGraw-Hill Kogakusha.

Harré, R., and Lamb, R. (eds) (1983) *The Encyclopedic Dictionary of Psychology*. Oxford: Blackwell.

Hays, W. L. (1963) *Statistics*. New York: Holt, Rinehart & Winston.

Jardine, N., and Sibson, R. (1971) *Mathematical Taxonomy*. Chichester: Wiley.

Jaspars, J. M. F. (1983) 'The task of social psychology: some historical reflections'. *British Journal of Social Psychology*, 22, 277–88.

Kirk, R. E. (1968) *Experimental Design: Procedures for the Behavioural Sciences*. Belmont, Cal.: Brooks Cole.

McDowall, D., McCleary, R., Meidinger, E. E., and Hay, R. A., Jr (1980) *Interrupted Time-Series Analysis. Quantitative Applications in the Social Sciences*, no. 21. Beverly Hills, Cal.: Sage.

Marriott, F. H. C. (1974) *The Interpretation of Multiple Observations*. London: Academic Press.

Maynard Smith, J. (1978) 'The evolution of behaviour'. *Scientific American*, 239 (3), 136–45.

Meehl, P. E. (1978) 'Theoretical risks and tabular asterisks: Sir Karl, Sir Ronald and the slow progress of soft psychology'. *Journal of Consulting and Clinical Psychology*, 46 (4), 806–34.

Mensch, A. (ed.) (1966) *Theory of Games: Techniques and Applications*. London: English Universities Press.

Messick, D. M. (ed.) (1968) *Mathematical Thinking in the Behavioural Sciences: Readings from Scientific American*. San Francisco, Cal.: Freeman.

Meyers, L. S., and Grossen, N. E. (1974) *Behavioural Research: Theory, Procedure and Design*. 2nd edn. San Francisco, Cal.: Freeman.

Neisser, U. (1967) *Cognitive Psychology*. New York: Appleton-Century-Crofts.

Ostrom, C. W., Jr (1978) *Time Series Analysis: Regression Techniques. Quantitative Applications in the Social Sciences*, no. 9. Beverly Hills, Cal.: Sage.

Platt, J. (1973) 'Social traps'. *American Psychologist*, 28 (8), 641–51.

Siegel, S. (1956) *Nonparametric Statistics for the Behavioural Sciences*. New York: McGraw-Hill.

Stahl, S. M., and Hennes, J. D. (1980) *Reading and Understanding Applied Statistics: A Self-Learning Approach*. 2nd edn. St Louis, Mo.: Mosby.

Tajfel, H., and Fraser, C. (1978) *Introducing Social Psychology*. Harmondsworth: Penguin.

Wilson, E. O. (1978) *On Human Nature*. Cambridge, Mass.: Harvard University Press.

# 2

# The analysis of meaning

## From causes to powers

In this chapter we turn away from statistics, dimensions, correlations, and so forth, to consider the more humanistic traditions of
research such as 'ethogenics', 'ethnomethodology' and 'symbolic
interactionism'. Ethogenics (literally, 'meaning-giving') is the science
which studies how action is rendered meaningful by the people who
do it and the people who observe it. Ethnomethodology, on the other
hand, is the study of the 'folk methodology' used by people in
everyday life for their own form of social science, enabling them to
create categories, measurements and estimates of the roles that they
and other people play, to gain a practical understanding of the nature
of institutions, and so on. Each of us is a sociologist in everyday life,
and ethnomethodology examines our private-life method for being
such. Finally, symbolic interactionism treats the interaction between
people as an exchange of symbols, and looks for the ways in which
action is rendered meaningful by the use of semantic schemes and
interpretative procedures. All the above schools of thought deal with
the idea of 'meaning' as the key property of action, and according to
Rom Harré, who founded and named the discipline of ethogenics,
the analysis of human action should be concerned primarily with
behavioural meaning. We shall try during the course of this chapter
to examine the ways in which such behavioural meaning can be
identified, classified, and used to help us find action structures in the
everyday world.

We shall introduce some of the arguments underlying Harré's critique of traditional experimental methodology, as a springboard into the analysis of behaviour and its meaning. Harré is a philosopher of science at Oxford University, and much of his work stems from his re-examination of the idea of explanation. What *is* it to explain things 'scientifically'? What sort of scientific explanation would be appropriate in the case of human action and its unfolding patterns over time? These are the sorts of questions to which we hope to suggest at least partial answers in the next few pages. A particularly good account of Harré's own work in this field can be found in his book *Social Being*.

*Figure 18*    The causal schema

A good starting-point for our purposes here is a simple conception of cause and effect, with all its problems and possible alternatives. Most of us use a causal framework to help us understand events in our daily lives, and it is normal to perceive events as the result of prior triggering conditions. However, it may not necessarily be a good thing to use the cause-and-effect model in the study of human action. Let us take an analogy with a simple physical system. Consider a match striking against a matchbox and igniting. The cause of the fire is the small amount of heat generated by the rubbing of the match against the box. For argument's sake we shall consider it to be an empirical law that matches will generally light in the same way when struck against the box. For this causal law to be much use to us, we ought to be able to claim that it is the property of all the matches in the box. But we cannot be sure this is true. Since we have not struck all the matches, we have not absolutely determined the validity of the law. We are faced with the problems of induction. Can we, in other words, generalize from the things that we have observed and measured, to the things that have not yet been observed or measured? There is another problem, relating to the nature and location of the law. If we say that the match has a tendency to light when struck, we have still not said how this information is contained within the match. Where does the relationship between cause and effect reside when the cause is not present, and therefore the effect is not being elicited? There must be something about the nature of the match which gives it a tendency towards that particular cause-and-effect relation, even when it has not been expressed by supplying the cause which would give it the opportunity to occur. These are standard problems with a simple conception of cause and effect, and they occur too in the simple stimulus–response conception of human action.

How are we to explain tendencies towards certain responses when certain stimuli occur, and how can we account for these tendencies as durable and stored properties of the organism in the *absence* of the appropriate stimuli? Further, can we be sure that the stimulus–response connection exists at all when the organism is inactive, and if it does exist, where is it? Surely it does not just manifest itself from nothing once the stimulus is presented! To overcome these objections Harré suggests the use of a slightly different explanatory framework, using the key concept of *powers*. Powers (or *tendencies*) are simply the capacities of things to act in certain ways under certain conditions (or *opportunities*).

Tendency–opportunity schemata are now becoming more popular in the natural sciences, while traditional cause-and-effect explanations are fading from prominence. The object of the exercise is to account for the *constitution* of objects and persons, in such a way that certain stimuli or conditions will be seen to result in certain behaviours, and furthermore in such a way that the tendency to show certain behaviours under specific circumstances can be seen as an enduring property of the organism *even when it is not currently being activated*. So, Harré thinks, we should replace the causal model of scientific explanation in psychology with the idea of *personal powers*. That is, we should think in terms of the capacities or the readinesses of a person or system to act, and of the properties that bestow these capacities. The action repertoire of a system consists of its various behaviours, in either the psychological or the broader sense (which would include the behaviour of any physical system), as modulated by changing *enabling conditions*. Notice that these enabling conditions are not to be seen as the 'causes' out of which the behaviour springs, but rather as the unlocking of a set of stored behavioural capacities, which were present all along in the form of a 'programme' or 'procedure' within the organism. There is no 'transfer of influence' between 'cause' and 'effect' in the sense that the kinetic energy of one object is imparted to another as they collide. The properties of the stimulus are in no way transmuted into the

properties of the response. If anything, the response takes its character from the nature and constitution of the organism, and it is there
that the explanation for it must be sought. The external circumstances are just the enabling conditions which release, on various
occasions, different facets of the stored system of tendencies.

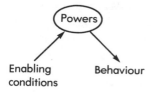

Figure 19    The tendency–opportunity schema

In the case of the match (see Figure 20), the story might now run
something like this. The match has a certain resting level of potential
chemical energy, and an obstacle to its release known as an 'energy
barrier'. The only way to release the stored bond-energy is to put in
*more* energy, so changing the molecular configurations within the
matchhead, and allowing an entropic process to start, in which the
energy stored in the orderly chemical structures is released as they
break down. In this case that would mean supplying an excitation
energy by rubbing the match against the matchbox. The friction
would produce heat and lift the energy level of the system over the
energy barrier, releasing the self-sustaining combustion process.

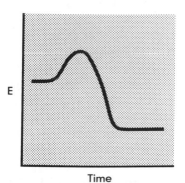

Time

Figure 20    Simple physical tendency–opportunity explanation

Of course this particular description is a far remove from the explanation of human action as such, but it does provide an example of how the powers and durable properties of an object might look in an explanatory schema, as opposed to a simple pairwise listing of circumstances and actions, or causes and effects.

It should be said, in fairness to the orthodox traditions of behavioural science, that this kind of explanation is already widely used in some parts of psychology, especially in the cognitive and physiological fields, where the behaviour of organisms is accounted for by the constitution of their 'software' and their 'hardware' respectively. The argument here is not for something totally new but for something that is not yet as widely accepted as it might be.

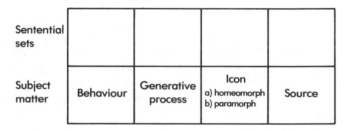

*Figure 21*    Stages in the discovery procedure (after Harré 1976a)

Figure 21 is a diagrammatic representation of Harré's discovery procedure for human action. He believes this schema to be a good description of the techniques actually used by natural scientists, unlike those normally put forward by philosophers of science.

There are two parts to the schema: first the 'sentential sets', which are sets of descriptions, formulae, equations, sentences, and so on; and secondly the 'subject matter' or things described by those sets. Although this is a neat philosophical distinction, we do not need to dwell on it here, but should just bear in mind the distinction to be drawn between what is described and the description which is offered of it. Turning to the subject matter, the starting-point in the discovery procedure is the behaviour of the system as it is observed. The aim of investigation is to understand the *generative process*, the source of the observed behaviour. This assumes a 'realist' philosophy of science, embodying the belief that it is possible to know the actual generative processes of the world if only indirectly, as opposed to the *instrumentalist* view, which makes the more modest claim that it is possible to invent theories which are useful in so far as they link and predict observations, but that any claim about the reality of un-observed entities and processes is unsupportable in principle. For now, we shall adopt the realist position. We are searching for the actual generative processes underlying behaviour, and we believe it is possible to uncover them.

Harré's approach starts from this point. He questions whether it is possible, however, to go directly from observed behaviour to under-lying processes. He suggests that practising scientists tend to find the idea rather absurd, even though it figures in some philosophies of science. How would one use behavioural data as a starting-point, and end up with results describing real generative processes, using some system of logical inference? Dismissing the inductivists' point of view, Harré suggests it is more productive to conceive of the process of discovery as being based on metaphor. This suggests that we should look first for an analogy for the behaviour we are investigating. This would be a different system (the 'source', in Harré's terms) which shared important characteristics with our object of study, but was better understood. From the source (of analogy) an 'icon' is then developed. This is an 'as if' model – a system of hypothetical processes which the real system behaves as if it embodied. The behaviour the icon would display is then inferred, to see if it matches that of the real system. If not, it is modified until it does, coming to resemble the real generative mechanism more and more closely in the process. The icon is not quite the same as the analogy. 'The analogy' usually refers to the business of drawing an analogy in general, or more specifically to the second system which is being used as a source of theoretical ideas. 'The icon' refers to that particular conception of the original object of enquiry which has been based on the properties of the second or analogical system. There are two forms of icon, *homeomorphs* and *paramorphs*. Homeomorphs are imaginary analogues of real systems taken from the *same* class as the thing being modelled, such as the study of one facet of human behaviour using an analogy with another facet of human behaviour.

A paramorph, on the other hand, is a model drawn from a different field. In studying the brain it is common to use cybernetic or computer models in this way.

Consider an example of the use of metaphor taken from the natural sciences. The pioneering work by Gregor Mendel in genetics fits nicely into the format described above. While working in his monastery garden in South Moravia, which was then part of Austria, Mendel observed certain 'behavioural' properties displayed by the sweet peas he studied. These included their inheritance ratios (the relative number of occurrences of certain filial traits for a given mixture of parental traits). He used an analogy with card games to help him understand what was going on. There were interesting resemblances between the regularities and structure of card games, and the simple regularities he was beginning to observe in the genetic properties of his plants. Some of the shared qualities of games and genes now seem very obvious – for instance, the fact that some sort of messages or particles are dealt out in indivisible chunks: discrete cards or genes cannot mix or have their value divided, but instead each represents a whole and particular quality, a case of all or nothing. One aspect of the analogy is less obvious – the origin of the idea of dominant and recessive genes. Two genes competing to determine a characteristic have an inherent dominance relation, meaning that one of them will prevail over the other if their specifications conflict. This is still a very significant genetic idea even today, and its inspiration rather surprisingly was the trump suits in some card games, whereby otherwise equal cards take unequal values when played off against each other.

In this case the icon was a paramorph. It was an analogy based on a *different* area of experience, with various properties imported and systematized to suggest how the actual genetic process might operate. Very often, as the icon comes to resemble the real generative process more and more, through conjecture, experiment and modification, the development of technology makes the previously hypothetical processes become things we can observe directly. So today we have electron microscopes and biochemical techniques, to confirm those early genetic conceptions at a molecular level, and to verify the chemical structure of the genes whose existence had originally been suggested by Mendel's imaginative use of metaphor.

This is an interesting instance of how an icon can operate in a simple, natural-scientific case, but how would it work in the analysis of human action? The source of analogy here, according to Harré, can be our everyday pre-scientific view of the system of human actions and meanings we are trying to explain. The role of the card game, in the genetic example, can be taken by the commonsense view of people, in the study of action. The rhetoric of needs, feelings, intentions and mental events, so often derided by psychologists for being 'unscientific', can be tentatively reintroduced in the status of an icon. Thus these commonsense understandings can be considered as part of a homeomorph, or an 'as if' model, for use in the explanation of human action, not because they are clearly correct, but as a basis for further theory and empirical test. This approach has particularly interesting applications in the analysis of deviant, antisocial or criminal behaviour. Typically a number of accounts of an event are available from participants, witnesses and victims, consisting of a mixture of reasons, justifications, excuses, complaints and accusations. Legal procedures have ways of sorting and assessing these statements, but psychological research methods by and large do not. One reason for this is the relative lack of credence that psychologists have given to people's knowledge of their own affairs, and the patterns of reasoning and choice underlying them. Another is the fear that we shall go too far, and seem gullible for taking seriously what is liable to be at least partly fabricated for the needs of the occasion. However, if we at least took seriously *in principle* that people can understand and report their own actions, in relation to their immediate subjective experience of their own mental life, and not relegate that possibility *out of hand* to some kind of scientific no man's land, then we should be in a position to use scientific tools to see when the ideas of lay psychology had been used credibly, and when they had not.

The task would then be to recombine the ideas in a sufficiently clear and rigorous way that their behavioural consequences could be deduced, checked against observation and experience, and modified where necessary. There is one technical difficulty with this, and that is how the fragments of everyday explanations can be pieced together to form a coherent structure which systematically predicts patterns of observable action – a kind of 'generative grammar' of human behaviour. This issue will be developed in the next chapter, where we deal with the relations between language and social behaviour, and the similar kinds of analysis which can be applied to both. The more formal schools of linguistics have embodied their theories in extremely systematic and coherent notational schemes called generative grammars, which attempt the recursive enumeration of all and only the sentences of a given language. In so far as the results match the linguists' intuitions about the sentences that would be well formed in that language, the grammar is said to achieve 'observational adequacy'. A similar view can be taken of the appropriate form, purpose and evaluation criteria of a predictive icon for natural action patterns.

The field of ethogenics is not, as people have often supposed, incompatible with reductive scientific explanation. One may progress here, as in other fields, from a rather broad level of description to an increasingly detailed characterization of the relevant substructures, dealing with progressively more mechanical and material embodiments of essentially the same process, just as one might reduce biological phenomena to physical or chemical descriptions, in some cases. From the ethogenic level of analysis, reduction leads to 'dramaturgy' and 'liturgy', the use of theatrical and liturgical metaphors to explain the structure of action. Thence the progression leads to systems theory, and on to cybernetics and finally to physiological explanations. Although we shall not attempt to deal here with the physiological level of explanation, in Chapter 4 we shall try to show how ideas from systems theory, cybernetics, computer modelling and artificial intelligence can offer us new conceptual schemata for the analysis of action systems.

So, equipped with the concepts of powers and enabling conditions, how are we to understand the nature of persons or the everyday 'social order'? How do human powers and capacities give rise to, and predispose us to, certain behavioural constructions? They can be thought of as a 'cognitive resource' operating within the actor, a template or procedure for the construction of action. This is the counterpart of the linguists' notion of 'competence', the set of idealized rules or knowledge that would be necessary for someone to produce and understand the linguistic performances we observe.

This knowledge, our lay theory of sociality, is what enables us to make sense of the world around us by recognition, classification and interpretation of events, occasions, institutions and people. To understand how action is rendered meaningful, therefore, we need to study the body of procedural knowledge with which this is achieved. Harré suggests that social competence is manifested in two ways: first in the form of spontaneous action (which is also what we have to explain) and secondly in the form of 'accounts'. Accounts are the explanations, stories, justifications, commentaries, and so on, issued in parallel with action, by which people present their actions for the comprehension and approval of others. It is the cross-connecting of action and accounts which is the core of ethogenic methodology, and

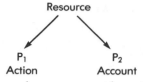

*Figure 22* Actions and accounts as evidence (after Harré 1976a)

the recommended way to uncover the common resources underlying both accounting and action.

Originally this theory was set out rather naïvely, suggesting that one could simply collect accounts of behaviour and take them to be veridical explanations as they stood. This seemed to make the assumption that what was said must be literally true. People could just tell you why they did what they did, and that was the end of the story. How easy research would be if that were all there was to it! However, recent formulations have presented a more elaborate and perhaps more realistic version of the idea. Now the cognitive re-source is seen as a very complex and variegated stock of knowledge, out of which both action and accounts have to be produced, although not necessarily from the *same part* of it. It is not that one can necessarily find a single area of the resource which gives rise to both the account and action in each instance. It may well be that one part of what somebody knows is fashioning their actions, and another part of what they know is fashioning their accounts, so a series of action-observing and account-gathering exercises would be needed to connect the pieces of this map into a sensible picture.

## The structure of action

Moving into the heartland of this topic, we need to establish what a description of action really is, whether offered of our own actions or other people's. Drawing again on a scheme of Harré's, there are three interrelated levels of activity description to consider. The lowest level is variously called 'behaviour' or 'movement', and is a physical characterization of activity, making reference to duration, forces, speeds, angles, and so on. By taking a video film of someone, and measuring limb positions, angles, and so forth, without reference to the likely purpose of the actions, or the conventional meanings normally attached to them, one would be producing a description at this lowest level in the 'act–action structure'. In case there is some

*Figure 23*    The act–action structure (after Harré 1976a)

confusion here, it should be pointed out that, in the discussion of act–action structures, terms like 'act' and 'action' are used with very specific and different meanings. Throughout the remainder of this book, however, these words are used in their more common and looser sense, in which they are more or less equivalent.

The next level introduces a semantic dimension into the description by considering 'actions', which are conventionalized sub-components of a larger, goal-directed unit called an 'act'. Thus a purely physical description of someone extending a hand, closing the fingers around the palm of somebody else's hand, and then oscillating the forearm up and down, is an item of behaviour, in this sense. However, the *action* is that of a handshake, and this in turn is part of a larger-scale and more deliberate event or *act*, which may be a greeting or the sealing of a bargain.

Finally, there needs to be some sort of organizing framework within which the actions and acts occur. Imagine the acts to be the parts of a more extended behavioural configuration or episode. We should need to know the procedures or rules by which the acts may be arranged sequentially into meaningful *strings*. To use an analogy, it is not particularly useful to discuss the concatenation of *morphemes* (grammatical elements like basic words and suffixes) to form potential sentences, unless you can specify which strings are members of the language and which are not. Similarly it is useless to talk about combinations of atoms into molecules, unless you are able to distinguish between two sets of combinations – the set that occurs as stable molecules, and the set that does not occur or is not stable. There has to be some form of dichotomous distinction between *well-formed* and *ill-formed* permutations, to underpin our explanation of how the various parts combine to create the many different types of wholes. In the analysis of action, this configurational or syntactic description serves as a way of defining the particular sets of episodes to be considered as characteristic of human beings.

Generally this approach fits into a holistic perspective. We are trying to explain what is manifest in the world by reference to what is concealed or latent, but we are *not* limited to analysing evident activity into its subcomponents. We can also pursue an increasingly global understanding of activity, by seeking to locate our original observations in broader contexts and activity structures.

We should be in the business, not only of taking apart observed phenomena to see what they are made of, but also of piecing them together to see what they are *part of*. This leads us to another hierarchical conception of the structure of action, again with three levels.

It is fair to assume that in human action, as in most things we are aware of, it is the middle range of scales and durations that are most apparent to us, and most prominent in our everyday conceptual schemata. There is a finer grain to things than we normally notice, and a coarser structure too, in action as in the physical world. Much of physical science is concerned with the substructure of entities as we experience them, but a few subjects, such as ecology or cosmology, are concerned with patterns too large for ordinary experience, the patterns of which our ordinary conceptions are themselves the subcomponents. The suggestion we want to advance here is that our everyday experience of action is similarly in the middle of the possible range of descriptive scales and scopes, and for this reason we call it the secondary (or evident) level of description.

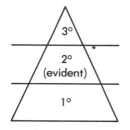

*Figure 24* Upward and downward explanation

Much of behavioural science attempts to reduce this to subcomponential (or primary) descriptions, while a neglected and attractive complement to this would be to explain by contextualizing, so as to produce higher-order or tertiary descriptions.

## The meaning of action

You will notice that in the description of act–action structures we introduced into the description of action the notion of 'semantic levels' – the idea of not just giving an objective physical description of events or behaviours in the world but also being able to overlay this with an understanding of their behavioural 'meaning'. This raises the issue of behavioural semantics. In what sense is behaviour meaningful, and what correspondence, if any, exists between the semantic structure of languages and the semantic structure of other forms of activity? We might ask if the relation between an event and what it represents is similar to the relation between linguistic tokens and their meanings. Ferdinand de Saussure, who is considered to be the originator of modern linguistics, suggested some interesting ways of looking at structure and meaning in language, and put forward the idea that language should be considered as just one part of a larger science of signs and their meanings, called *semiology* or *semiotics*. He felt that the structure of language consisted of two classes of relations between words. The first class he called 'syntagmatic relations' – the way in which words (or other elements) combine over time into larger organizational structures such as clauses, sentences or paragraphs. These are the sentence-forming relations which resemble the modern conception of syntax. The second class is the 'paradigmatic relations' (which Saussure had originally called associative), and these define how certain words can be associated by form or meaning, or by playing the same role in a sentence, for example. These words are bound together by their similarity of morphology, meaning or function or, to put it another way, by their correspondence of syntactic role.

Taken together, the two sets of relations, syntagmatic and paradigmatic, form a kind of matrix, the *Saussurean grid*, which makes a good foundation for the analysis of action structure and meaning, even though it has long been superseded by much more elaborate theories in the field of language itself.

These two 'axes' of internal meaning could prove useful in the analysis of some unfamiliar ritual, for example. The paradigmatic dimensions would consist of the groupings of sounds, gestures, utterances, expressions, emblems, and so on, which could stand in for one another, and serve one another's purposes as the ceremony unfolded, rather as the printed order of service in church provides for alternative forms of words to be used interchangeably at various points. The syntagmatic analysis would then consist of the description of the *sequential* relations governing the proceedings, and the possible permutations and constraints which allow quite different configurations of action, serving quite different purposes, to be assembled from the same basic units.

As an aside, it is interesting to note that much the same thinking has a long and productive history in the natural sciences too. When Mendeleev was first compiling the periodic table of the chemical elements, showing how with increasing atomic number the same chemical properties kept recurring in a cyclical fashion at about every eighth chemical element in the series, he used much the same reasoning. Elements could be cast into families (paradigmatic structures) having equivalent combinatorial properties (called valency in chemistry, hence the particular aptness of the word *equivalent* or *equi-valent*) by grouping together all those that formed the same-shaped crystals when combined with the same selection of other elements. Here the crystal lattices were serving as the syntagmatic structures, and their similarity of form when certain elements were substituted for each other was evidence of the similar combinatorial properties of the substitutable items. It was on this basis that the family grouping of elements on which much of modern chemistry rests was built up. An example of such a chemical family is the group of so-called 'halide' elements, which includes fluorine, chlorine, bromine and iodine.

It is important, if a clear structure is to emerge from the Saussurean grid and its subsequent sequence analysis (outlined in Chapter 3), that here too the paradigmatic structure be derived specifically from the partitioning of the universe of events or units into *equivalence classes*, according to their commutability within well-formed structures. That is to say that the overall analysis of structure will work only if it is based on a typology of events according to their similarity of combinatorial properties, and that is best determined by their 'swapability' in and out of each other's contexts. Taking paradig-

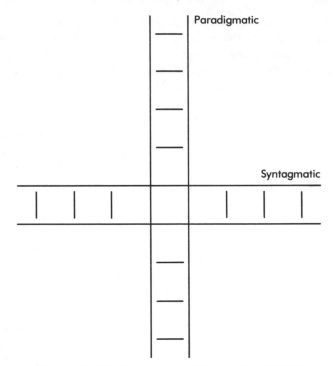

*Figure 25*   The Saussurean grid (after Harré 1976a)

matic relations in this *specific* sense, therefore, both the structure of language and the structure of action systems can be defined according to the two sets of relations – syntagmatic relations specifying the combination of units into larger constructions over time, and paradigmatic relations dictating the equivalent sets of units on which syntagmatic rules operate. For instance, in the sentence 'The cat sat on the mat', the syntagmatic relations determine how the words fit together, and the paradigmatic relations would allow the word 'cat' to be replaced by 'dog', or any other noun, which is how nouns came to be a grammatical category. Of course, 'cat' could not be replaced by words like 'slowly', 'blue', 'over' or 'by'. There are many types of words that cannot replace 'cat', and it is by looking at the classes of words that *are* mutually substitutable that one defines the syntactic classes or parts of speech on which the grammatical description of the language is based. One can equally well apply this logic to the elements in an action structure, by considering which of them are substitutable, either in principle, or because they are observed to appear in similar contexts to one another. A classification according to the equivalence of events in their functions and combinatorial properties can then be made, and between these paradigmatic types the syntagmatic relations can then be examined.

The kinds of event meaning provided by the consideration of syntagmatic and paradigmatic relations are both 'internalist'. They are semantic structures that only relate one part of the 'interior' of the language or action system to something else which is also 'inside' that system. It is rather like looking up words in a dictionary. What you find are further words which could also be looked up in the dictionary. In a sense you are going around in circles. This is in the nature of internalist semantic schemes. They refer one part of the scheme for its meaning to another part of the same scheme, and do not relate it to anything outside that particular system.

We have looked at two internalist types of meaning given by syntagmatic and paradigmatic relations between events. There are two more to consider, which are both 'externalist' and refer *outside* the system. The first of these is the externalist semantic which is most common in language (although less so in the case of action) and is called the 'referential semantic'. This is the aspect of meaning by which something within the signalling or behavioural system *stands for*, or betokens, something outside – such as a word representing an object in the world, or an assertion standing for a state of affairs, and so on. Usually behaviour cannot be said to have that sort of meaning, but there are cases, particularly in ritual, where behaviour has a symbolic meaning of exactly this kind.

The fourth and final form of meaning we need to look at is also externalist and is known as the 'prescriptive semantic'. This is the aspect of behaviour which sets down instructions, prescriptions and obligations for the future. It is a common aspect of the meaning of action that it can hold implicit obligations and expectations for oneself and others in the future. For instance, when one starts to develop a friendship with someone, there are many levels of meaning to the events which occur, some of which have to do with the commitments or rules which are laid down for the future growth of that relationship.

All theories of meaning, whether in language or behaviour, have difficulty dealing with the effects of context. Since words and actions depend in part on their context for their meaning to be determined, a satisfactory theory of meaning should be able to capture the various permutations of meaning given to the same event or word by different contexts. This is easier said than done. In the case of language, the problem, though not solved, is at least fairly limited. Most words, for instance, can be given some kind of definition without reference to context. In the case of behavioural meaning the problem is far worse. Very few actions have any significance when considered out of context, and the range of meanings that the same act could assume in different contexts can be almost limitless. What, for example, is the significance of someone walking across a room to pick up a magazine? In a dentist's waiting room it might be a sign of nervous impatience; after an argument it might be a display of sulky inattention to the rest of the family; or while the television set is on it could be the means of choosing a programme. In other circumstances the same overt event might be the preliminary to buying a car; a quick check of the week's horoscope; or the selection of a recipe for the evening meal. The possibilities are endless. To make matters worse, the problem is also circular. Each event gets its meaning from the context, but the context is no more than a configuration of further events and circumstances, each dependent for meaning on *its* context. It seems to be a tangle with no loose ends from which it can be unravelled.

There is no complete answer to this, and schemes for the semantic analysis of action all tend to run into the problem at some stage or other, as we shall see. A partial answer does exist, though, in the use of theory-driven rather than data-driven research procedures. In a study based on proper theoretical foundations, the theory provides the purpose for the observations and the context for their interpretation. It is *because* a certain theory implies that observation X will be possible if and only if it is true that there is any scientific reason for trying to observe X. Furthermore, this provides the grounds for interpreting X, the significance of which is that it supports the theory. This is a general formulation of the problem, which includes interpretations of X in terms of actors' meanings if the underlying theory is a theory of meaning and motivation; but it also applies in other cases where the theory is of a different kind, and so too is the resulting significance of the observations it suggests. For the sake of simplicity this argument has been couched in *verificationist* terms, as if scientific theories are proved by some observations and disproved by others. In fact it is not so straightforward, and a strong case can be made for the *falsificationist* view that there are observations which can disprove a theory, but no observations which could possibly prove one, once and for all (e.g. Popper 1972a). This is partly because of the impossibility of generalizing from a finite number of observations to the general case, and partly because a theory implies that certain observations could be made, but not vice versa. The logical consequences of this are that the falsity of the implied observations entails the falsity of the theory, but the validity of the observations does not entail the validity of the theory. (Generally, in any sound deductive system, false conclusions indicate false premises, but true conclusions do not indicate true premises.)

## Types of explanation

Having provided a brief outline of four different perspectives on meaning, we shall now return to the issue of causes and explanations. Aristotle proposed four classes of 'causation', called *material, final, efficient* and *formal* causes. We shall consider each in turn as possible formats for action explanation, in ascending order of importance for our purpose. 'Material causes', rather like powers, have to do with the (usually physical) constitution of a system. To give a concrete example, if someone said 'My notes have just reminded me, you should read Smith's latest book', then the material causes of the statement would be found in the apparatus of speech, such as the speaker's lungs and vocal chords, and their attendant pressures and vibrations. These are the physically necessary conditions, or the material causes, of any utterance. However, in the same example, the 'final cause' would concern the purpose behind the words. Perhaps the speaker had made a deal with the author, and stood to earn money on every copy of the book that was sold, or else genuinely believed it was so worthwhile that it should be widely read. In any case, there were motives behind the speech, and there was some future state of affairs towards which the actions were supposed to lead. So the final cause is a *teleological* or reason-oriented explanation. 'Efficient causation' is the familiar 'billiard ball' conception of cause and effect, such as a prior event which had triggered off the remark we want to explain. In this case, since the speaker said 'My notes have just reminded me . . .', it seems to be some information in the notes that was the triggering factor which gave rise to that type of utterance at that moment. The notes, though, did not contain a specific stimulus to a specific utterance; they only provided a triggering event for a general class of behaviour. We have still not accounted for the fact that the sentence took its particular form and that the syntax was organized in a certain way, nor have we explained the modulation of pitch, or the tone of voice that was used. None of these was a property of the notes, or of the intention behind the act, or of the material equipment of speech. For an explanation of these things we need to look at Aristotle's last type of cause, the 'formal cause', in order to understand why the remark took one particular form as opposed to another. In this case the formal cause would be the speaker's knowledge of the language and of the social conventions for making recommendations in this particular culture.

Ethogenics places special emphasis on formal causes because they are often neglected in behavioural analysis, and are concerned with the beliefs and rules which guide and shape action, given that something else, an efficient cause, has initiated it. This issue, the control of the *forms* of action, which other things control the *occurrence* of, is central to the ethogenic programme of research.


## Life sentences

Perhaps all this theorizing will fall into place if we examine an example of the practical application of ethogenic analysis. The study we shall describe was quite mature before the investigator (the Belgian prison psychiatrist and personality psychologist, Jean-Pierre de Waele) came across Harré's work, after which they collaborated for some time, realizing they had been talking about the same type of ideas and explanations. In that sense the example is not *based on* ethogenic analysis, but is consistent with it.

The study concerns the biography of murderers, and the documentation of the singular life events which seem to shape and influence them. The *psycho-biographies* in question were constructed partly to try to understand the difference between two kinds of murderers, those who will not commit murder again, and those who will murder again and again.

Of course, being able to discriminate between the two types is of great importance when it comes to making parole decisions. This method of investigation aims to provide a *process* model of how and why the original murder took place, thereby predicting the likelihood of a future occurrence. This is in contrast to the 'actuarial' approach to parole decisions, which uses statistics on recidivism as a function of age, sex, class, previous criminal record, and so on.

The study team worked with convicted murderers who had committed an average of two to three murders each, in the special-purpose wing of a Belgian prison. There were four types of enquiry making up the overall study, and they were distinguished by two dichotomies. The investigations were 'synchronic' or 'diachronic', and 'person-centred' or 'situation-centred'. (Synchronic studies produce a static view of a phenomenon in the here and now, while diachronic studies show its structure over a period of time. In this case the synchronic enquiries tended to investigate the prisoner while inside gaol, whereas the diachronic investigations looked into the prisoner's life history up to the time of imprisonment.) We shall now describe the procedures used to elicit the four different types of information.

|                    | Synchronic   | Diachronic      |
|--------------------|--------------|-----------------|
| Person-centred     | PCS          | Autobiography   |
| Situation-centred  | Observation  | Social enquiry  |

*Figure 26*   The four parts of de Waele's psycho-biographical method

The synchronic, person-centred study employed 'problem-and-conflict situations' (or PCSs). The investigators devised ways of frustrating the prisoner almost beyond endurance, in order to see how he reacted to certain kinds of psychological stress. They set up simple mechanical tasks, such as reaching for a rose and retrieving it from a slim vase on the opposite side of the room. However, the prisoner was not allowed to cross the intervening space, and had to utilize some rather unhelpful equipment, like pages of a newspaper, string and boxes of old tools. Some of these tasks are possible, and others are not, but generally it is not clear to the subject at the outset which is which. In the case of the 'rose test', the prisoner's goal is to find three separate ways of retrieving the rose. The equipment provided allows it to be retrieved fairly readily. Usually within a short period of time the prisoner finds two methods of retrieval. However, the investigator then systematically disallows any third solution, using any pretext for this, however transparent. Maybe the third solution was too similar to the first two, or the prisoner had misused the equipment, or some additional rule had been remembered which should have been mentioned before. The prisoners continue to struggle to find the third solution. They take the task seriously, because they know that good behaviour and good task performance may contribute to parole decisions. In this way prisoners can be kept within a chalked circle for hours on end, desperately trying to find the final solution. Not surprisingly, they become progressively more upset, frustrated, anxious and hostile. During this period of emotional upheaval, the prisoners produce various kinds of associational material, emotional language, projections on to the equipment, and so on. Sometimes they attribute sinister motives to the people around them, consider the objects they have been given as deliberately counter-productive, and so forth. As this goes on, the investigators gather information about certain aspects of the prisoner's mentality, and his way of coping with stress.

The next method used to gain information about the murderer is his autobiography, which makes up the the diachronic, person-centred aspect of the study. The prisoner writes and rewrites his life story in collaboration with the investigators, and in so doing is forced to rethink and re-articulate his past history. Obviously this is a very reactive method, and its very reactivity is a deliberate part of the exercise. The investigators are influencing, and helping to change, the prisoner's view of himself and his past, as well as to document his original and changing conceptions. As such, this aspect of the investigation can play a therapeutic, as well as a fact-gathering, role. Thirdly, the prisoners were observed within the prison by specially trained prison guards, to help create a picture of the murderer as he currently lived and related to those around him. This was the synchronic, situation-centred study. Lastly, a survey was undertaken by social workers, of specific aspects of the prisoner's past life. This was the diachronic, situation-centred study.

Each specialist who had examined a particular aspect of the case presented various possible findings, including the true ones, in a multiple-choice format, to other investigators from the same discipline who had worked on related aspects of the case. The extent to which each finding could be inferred by someone who only had knowledge of different findings provided a measure of the coherence and intelligibility of the picture that was building up. After the sociologists, the psychologists and the psychiatrists as sub-teams had each reached a consensus, the same process was repeated between the sub-teams, to check the consistencies and cross-links running through the case as a whole.

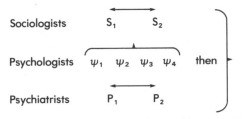

*Figure 27*   Cross-checking the case within and between disciplines

Having given an outline of the technique used by de Waele, we shall now consider an actual case history, and the findings produced by the application of these methods. It concerns a Belgian man called 'Henry', aged about 30, who has already been in prison for thirteen years. The research team had to go back two generations to unravel his family history.

In the beginning there were two separate married couples. One couple had a son, and the other couple had a daughter. One partner in each marriage died, leaving a widow with a daughter and a widower with a son. The widow and widower met, married, and soon found they were expecting a baby. This event meant that the wife would have to go into hospital. The parents felt it would be improper for the two children by their previous marriages, who were now teenage step-siblings, to be left alone for any length of time in the house. It was decided by the parents and local priest that the children should be married, to avoid a scandal. This marriage took place and later produced two sons. It was not a happy marriage. The husband took to drinking and the wife became depressed. Both the sons identified with their mother, and wanted to find a solution to her distress.

When the murder took place, the elder son, who is the subject of this case history, was 16 and the younger one was 12. Henry, the older brother, was an interesting character. He had a very vivid fantasy life, in which he saw himself as a kind of James Bond figure. He thought up schemes for great adventures, and seemed to be devoid of any normal sense of conscience. He would undertake actions on pragmatic grounds regardless of their consequences for other people, and when the two boys set about deciding how they could relieve their mother's plight they decided to kill their father. They looked into the practicalities of this, and decided it was rather a tall order for them, so instead they decided to kidnap a schoolfriend and demand a ransom for him. With the ransom money, they and their mother would leave, their father would remain behind with his bottle, and all would be well. This is what they set out to accomplish, but again they realized that to hold a friend of theirs to ransom, to get the money, and to let him go in a way which would not incriminate them, was beyond their means. So now they resolved that it would be a faked kidnapping, and that as soon as they got hold of their friend they would kill him.

The child they chose was a rather pathetic lad. He was about 13, obese, spotty, lonely, and so desperately in need of friendship that he was prepared to tolerate almost any abuse to have the attention of these two boys. They used that need for friendship as the basis for their murder plot.

In the first stage the older boy told his mother that he needed to borrow 3000 Belgian francs for a scheme which would help them all, but that he could not tell her what it was. She refused, but being a very dependent sort of woman (throughout the whole story she was more dependent on her son than he was on her) she gave in later that day, and gave him the 3000 francs without question. He took a train to a nearby town, where he bought a harpoon gun. He returned home, gave his mother the change, and said that he had set his scheme in motion. The two brothers then invited the young school-friend to come round to play. Of course, they did not want him to leave any traces, so they said that their father did not approve of his coming to play, and that he must be sure not to come on his bicycle and leave it outside their garden gate. (Throughout the plot there is an interesting mixture of juvenile ideas and very sinister adult reasoning.) So the young lad came over, the three boys played in the back garden, and during the course of the game, Henry jumped out from behind a bush and shot his friend with the harpoon gun. It did not kill him; the harpoon only went through his arm, and Henry was able to break it and extract it. The young friend, in his desperation for friendship, was then persuaded that this was all in the nature of good clean fun, that he should think nothing more of it, and that he should come back the next day to play again – which he did. The next day he was to be killed in earnest.

The game this time was Nazi soldiers, and the brothers took him up to the attic of their house, tied him to a chair with electrical flex, and set about clubbing him to death with a gun butt. In the course of all this the doorbell rang, and the family doctor arrived at the house to visit the boys' mother, who was ill in the next-door room. The two boys ceased their 'interrogation', went downstairs, let in the doctor, chatted to him, took him up to see their mother in the next room, ushered him out again, and then went back to carry on with their game. This time they finally succeeded in clubbing their friend to death. They wrapped the body in a roll of carpet, using one of two carpet offcuts which were in the attic, and went on down to lunch. They had a nasty moment when their father said over lunch: 'Oh, it's the local flag day today. I must pop up to the attic and get out our family flag. I think we'll hang it from the house.' The boys were afraid, of course, that the body would be discovered, but the crisis passed and the body remained undisturbed.

That night the two brothers crept out of the house under cover of darkness and took the body to a neighbour's garden, where it was put down the shaft of a well. On the way home they were discovered by their parents, who had noticed they were out of the house. They tried to spin a yarn about how the younger brother had an important test at school the next day, and Henry had taken him out for a walk to calm his nerves, but the parents were unconvinced. The murdered boy had been missing since lunchtime, and very soon his body was discovered in the well of the neighbour's garden. The police found the other half of the carpet in the brothers' attic, and the case was cleared up very quickly. The brothers were committed for trial.

Very little of this story came out at the trial. The legal proceedings took their normal course. The rights and wrongs of the matter were determined to the satisfaction of the law. The younger boy went into care, and the older boy went to prison with recommendations for psychiatric treatment. The story as we have reported it remained largely unknown to the authorities, and it was only later that it was pieced together by the team investigating the pattern of motives and plans behind the murder.

This is only a very brief outline of the story. The full case report is a thousand-page document detailing the complete life-course of this individual, his interests, his fantasies, what he found interesting and uninteresting in life, what he was like since infancy, how he reacted to the problem-and-conflict situations, and so on. The case as a whole has a coherent and consistent framework, which was built up using what the team call their 'defocusing strategy'. That is to say, they did not allow themselves to know the facts of the murder when they were piecing together the other parts of the biography. They assembled the whole thing with just one bit missing, rather like a car without an engine, and then finally revealed to themselves the facts of the murder, and fitted it into the position in the biographical framework which it was supposed to occupy. They checked in various ways for the consistency of this fit, and satisfied themselves that they had an accurate account of the events that had taken place, and the reasons for them.

Henry is still in his prison cell. He is entirely unrepentant, and he is still fantasizing about the exciting things one can do with harpoons and machine guns. He has gruesome posters all over his walls, and his mother still comes to the prison every week so that *he* can comfort *her*. Even though he is in gaol for murder, and will probably stay there for the rest of his life, his mother, although apparently free and independent, still feels she must turn to him for support. She visits him every week, so that he can advise her, and together they dream dreams and make elaborate plans for how they are going to transform their future, and be together in the years to come. As far as the research team can determine, Henry's mentality is entirely unchanged. The sorts of reasoning that led him to murder so 'rationally' and so cold-bloodedly are still with him, and while that remains the case he will stay in his prison cell in Brussels.

There are a number of other lessons to be drawn from this story, of which the scientific ones are the most relevant for our purpose. There are lessons in the nature of the explanation which was arrived at, and in the nature of the procedure which was used to elicit it. We cannot go into them all here, but this brief account does give the flavour of a quite different, and yet systematic, mode of investigation being used to explain an elaborate and important pattern of human action. In particular this analysis illustrates how the concepts and terms of ordinary commonsense mentalism can be used quite rigorously in a form of psychological enquiry which is richer and more relevant than most laboratory studies, but is none the less thorough.

In summary, it seems that the understanding of complex action systems involves making conceptual models, homeomorphic or paramorphic icons, whose mechanism the real system behaves *as if* it possessed. Often these models involve networks of mathematical or logical relationships, rather than images of physical machinery with levers or wires. In this sense the processes governing action can be envisaged as configurations of software rather than hardware, just as many of a computer's properties can best be understood from its programs rather than its circuitry. The two branches of cognitive science where this style of explanation is well advanced are the field of language and linguistics on the one hand, and on the other, the world of artificial intelligence and computer simulation. We shall be discussing some of the contributions of these two areas to a general theory of human action in Chapters 3 and 4.

## Further reading

Atkinson, J. M., and Drew, P. (1979) *Order in Court: The Organisation of Verbal Interaction in Judicial Settings*. London: Macmillan.

Axline, V. (1971) *Dibs: In Search of Self*. Harmondsworth: Penguin.

Batson, C. D. (1972) 'Linguistic analysis and psychological explanation of the mental'. *Journal for the Theory of Social Behaviour*, 2 (1), 37–59.

Berenson, F. M. (1981) *Understanding Persons: Personal and Impersonal Relationships*. Hassocks: Harvester.

Bowlby, J. (1979) *The Making and Breaking of Affectional Bonds*. London: Tavistock.

Cicourel, A. V. (1973) *Cognitive Sociology*. Harmondsworth: Penguin.

Clarke, D. D. (1983) 'Emotion and personality'. In R. Harré and R. Lamb (eds), *The Encyclopedic Dictionary of Psychology*. Oxford: Blackwell.

Dennett, D. C. (1978) *Brainstorms*. Hassocks: Harvester.

Freud, S. (1962) *Two Short Accounts of Psychoanalysis*. Harmondsworth: Penguin.

Garfinkel, H. (1967) *Studies in Ethnomethodology*. Englewood Cliffs, NJ: Prentice-Hall.

Gergen, K. J. (1973) 'Social psychology as history'. *Journal of Personality and Social Psychology*, 26, 309–20.

Goffman, E. (1971) *Relations in Public*. Harmondsworth: Penguin.

Harré, R. (1975) *Causal Powers*. Oxford: Blackwell.

Harré, R. (1976a) 'The constructive role of models'. In L. Collins (ed.), *The Use of Models in the Social Sciences*. London: Tavistock.

Harré, R. (ed.) (1976b) *Life Sentences*. Chichester: Wiley.

Harré, R. (1977) 'The ethogenic approach: theory and practice'. In L. Berkowitz (ed.), *Advances in Experimental Social Psychology*, 10. New York: Academic Press.

Harré, R. (1979) *Social Being*. Oxford: Blackwell.

Harré, R. (1983) *Personal Being*. Oxford: Blackwell.

Harré, R., Clarke, D. D., and Carlo, N. de (1985) *Motives and Mechanisms: An Introduction to the Psychology of Action*. London: Methuen.

Hofstadter, D. R., and Dennett, D. C. (1981) *The Mind's I: Fantasies and Reflections on Self and Soul*. Hassocks: Harvester.

Hudson, L. (1972) *The Cult of the Fact*. London: Jonathan Cape.

Langer, S. K. (1967) *Mind: An Essay on Human Feelings*. Baltimore, Md: Johns Hopkins University Press.

Maslow, A. (1972) *The Farther Reaches of Human Nature*. Harmondsworth: Penguin.

Morton, A. (1980) *Frames of Mind*. Oxford: Clarendon.

Peacocke, C. (1979) *Holistic Explanation: Action, Space, Interpretation*. Oxford: Clarendon.

Popper, K. R. (1972a) *The Logic of Scientific Discovery*. 2nd edn. London: Hutchinson.

Popper, K. R. (1972b) *Objective Knowledge*. London: Oxford University Press.

Ross, L. (1977) 'The intuitive psychologist and his shortcomings'. In L. Berkowitz (ed.), *Advances in Experimental Social Psychology*, 10. New York: Academic Press.

Sheehy, G. (1981) *Pathfinders*. Toronto: Bantam.

Smedslund, J. (1978) 'Bandura's theory of self efficacy: a set of commonsense theorems'. *Scandinavian Journal of Psychology*, 19, 1–14.

Stone, G. P., and Farberman, H. R. (1970) *Social Psychology through Symbolic Interaction*. Waltham, Mass.: Ginn-Blaisdell.

Storr, A. (1960) *The Integrity of the Personality*. Harmondsworth: Penguin.

Storr, A. (1973) *Jung*. Glasgow: Fontana.

Storr, A. (ed.) (1983) *The Essential Jung*. London: Fontana.

Strawson, P. F. (1964) 'Intention and convention in speech acts'. *Philosophical Review*, 73, 439–60. In P. F. Strawson (ed.), *Logico-Linguistic Papers*. London: Methuen, 1971.

Strickland, L. H., Aband, F. E., and Gergen, K. J. (1976) *Social Psychology in Transition*. New York: Plenum.

Tomkins, S. S. (1965) 'Affect and the psychology of knowledge'. In S. S. Tomkins and C. E. Izard (eds), *Affect, Cognition and Personality*. New York: Springer.

Totman, R. (1980) 'The incompleteness of ethogenics'. *European Journal of Social Psychology*, 10 (1), 17–40.

Turner, R. (ed.) (1973) *Ethnomethodology*. Harmondsworth: Penguin.

Van Der Post, L. (1976) *Jung and the Story of our Time*. London: Hogarth.
Waele, J.-P. de, and Harré, R. (1979) 'Autobiography as a psychological method'. In G. Ginsberg (ed.), *Emerging Strategies in Social Psychological Research*. Chichester and New York: Wiley.

# 3

# Language and action

## Action as language

In this chapter we shall explore some of the connections between language and action. To do this we have borrowed ideas from linguistics, linguistic pragmatics, sociolinguistics, conversation analysis and ethology. These areas will be explained briefly, and a description given of the role they can play in the study of action.

There are two senses in which language and action are related. First, language forms a part of most elaborate activities, so it can be seen as a subcomponent part of the texture of action. The second and less apparent relationship (which might seem like a contradiction of the first) is that action can be understood in terms of a theory of organization for which linguistic analysis is the model. In other words, language is not only a part of but also an *analogue* of the structure of human action. From this point of view, action structures are to be seen as the parts of a larger, language-like system. We can then invoke a general scheme of explanation for studying them, using concepts like syntax, semantics, generative rules, criteria of adequacy, and so on – especially since action structures, like linguistic structures, are largely a matter of the temporal order of events or signals. (Language or action *systems* we take to mean something more general, including not only the structures themselves but the entire network of processes, consequences and values within which they occur.) The point is that the theories which are normally applied to language can be applied to other forms of action, or, to put it another way, the wider world of action can be encapsulated within an extended theory of linguistics. That is what is meant by (one use of) the term 'structuralism'.

The first of these relationships highlights the role language plays in action, and could be said to represent the social scientist's conception of language, in which language is fitted into explanatory models of social behaviour containing concepts such as class, social skill and power. This perspective has accounted for much of the work in the field of sociolinguistics. The second relationship, on the other hand, might be seen as capturing the linguist's notion of the social world, in which action is examined in terms of linguistic methods and concepts.

Let us consider some fundamental ideas in linguistics, in order to assess the connections between language and behaviour in more detail. Linguistics is a very complex subject, and there is not enough space to do it justice here, so for now we shall consider just a few key areas.

A central figure in modern linguistics is Noam Chomsky, a professor at the Massachusetts Institute of Technology (MIT). Many of the ideas we shall be dealing with date from 1957, when Chomsky published his famous book *Syntactic Structures*. Until that time most linguists had attempted to analyse the structuring principles underlying fragments of spoken or written language by dividing them into their component parts. Chomsky's former tutor Zellig Harris, and later Chomsky himself, argued that analysing texts in great detail in search of their key organizing principles was not the right approach, and that instead linguists should start with hypothetical structuring principles, and look for evidence of their correctness. Harris and Chomsky suggested the use of 'generative rules' which could be used to formulate what amounts to a simulation of the language, called a generative grammar. This requires a set of rigorously specified axiomatic rules, from which all sentences in a language and their meanings can be deduced. This style of analysis has since been likened to the development of the theorem-proving systems used in mathematics and logic, and some of the notations and terms in generative linguistics were based on the conventions for describing theorem-proving systems.

Before turning to the specific parts of a generative grammar, such as 'surface structure', 'deep structure' and 'transformational rules' we shall run through a simple account of one basic issue in linguistic analysis. Any satisfactory theory of language (or action) must deal with the question of how form and function are related. One could argue that the task of the speaker and hearer respectively is to turn 'meaning' into some transmissible form – that is into particular combinations of words and phrases – and the reverse. In this way meaning is transported in a message, compiled by the speaker, to the hearer, who somehow manages to decode the message and recover the original meaning. One of the crucial properties of language is that words are combined under rules which systematically relate sequential permutations to different meanings. By knowing these rules, or something like them, the speaker and hearer are both enabled to communicate. Because of their central role in the functioning of language, we must know *what* systematic relationships exist between the different ways of combining words into sentences, and the meanings that those sentences would convey to a native speaker, or in other words the principles of relationships between form and function. Take, for example, the sentence 'They were visiting firemen.' This is a member of an important class of sentences because of its ambiguity. It could mean that some people went along to visit some firemen, or that some firemen went on a visit. The existence of ambiguity such as this raises a central problem in understanding the mapping from form to meaning in language. It is clearly *not* a simple one-to-one relationship. There is no direct correspondence between every possible sentence and its one and only meaning. Even though many sentences do convey only one meaning, a satisfactory account of the relationship between form and meaning *must* deal with the existence of ambiguous sentences where one form has several meanings, and also the cases where one meaning can take several forms. Because of this complication we need some sort of theoretical procedure to specify the relationship between form and function.

In Figure 28 there is a sentence, and tree diagrams above and below it. (Because the sentence is ambiguous, *two* trees are needed; normally one would be enough.) These tree diagrams represent what is called the 'surface structure' of the sentence. The surface structure, roughly speaking, is the grouping of the words. In the case of this sentence one interpretation reads 'They *were visiting* firemen', and the second reads 'They were *visiting firemen*'. The surface structures, as distinguished by the two tree diagrams, have disambiguated the sentence, and the origin of the ambiguity has been identified. But

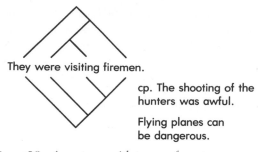

They were visiting firemen.

cp. The shooting of the
hunters was awful.

Flying planes can
be dangerous.

*Figure 28*    A sentence with two surface structures

unfortunately not all sentences are ambiguous as a result of their having two surface structures. For instance 'The shooting of the hunters was awful' and 'Flying planes can be dangerous' are also ambiguous, but no matter how hard you try to disambiguate them by redescription of their surface structure, the meaning will not become more specific. For this, and other more technical reasons, the suggestion was put forward by Chomsky that we should consider another level of grammatical or syntactic organization underlying the apparent sentence structure. This unseen aspect of linguistic organization was called the 'deep structure' of sentences. The process of mapping from the semantic representations (or meanings) of a sentence to its single surface structure needs to be done in two stages in the case of a sentence with deep-structural ambiguity. For each deep structure there is by definition one, and only one, corresponding meaning, or semantic representation – which is to say that deep structures and semantic representations differ in type but not in number. On the other hand, deep and surface structures are of the same type (syntactic descriptions) but can exist in many-to-one and one-to-many correspondence. So, rather neatly, the two differences between surface structure and meaning, differences of type and differences of number, are separated out with a new kind of sentence description, the deep structure, acting as a staging post in between.

The above ideas have taken us a little closer to an understanding of grammar-writing and the representation of language in the form of generative rules. We can now look at a simple grammar (a set of rules for the recursive enumeration of the sentences in a language), which consists of the following elements: a terminal vocabulary ($V_T$), a non-terminal vocabulary ($V_N$), a set of productions or generative rules (P) and a start symbol (S). The terminal vocabulary, as its name suggests, is the final output of the grammar – the pieces of the sentences themselves. The non-terminal vocabulary consists of concepts that are manipulated during the process of formally reproducing sentence structures, such as *noun phrase, verb phrase*, and so on. These items are acted upon by the rules, but do not appear in the final output. The productions are the generative rules themselves, and the start symbol is simply the initial state of the system of rules, the axiom from which all the derivations begin. These grammatical descriptions are highly formalized, and they emphasize the role of language as a system in which meanings are encoded into sentences, and then transformed by the hearer back into meanings.

$$G = <V_T, V_N, P, S>$$

*Figure 29*    The components of a simple grammar

Generative grammars provide an analytical framework for language which can be used to describe forms of action besides language *per se*. Generative grammars represent and reproduce structures by using rules of substitution which allow abstract and general specifications of a pattern, such as a sentence, to be transformed into increasingly concrete and detailed descriptions, which may then be matched to real or hypothetical examples of that type of action or language, to discover how well the rules have performed.

An early example of a *behaviour* grammar may be found in Marshall's re-analysis of data collected by Fabricius and Jansson, describing copulation in pigeons. Figure 30 shows the rewrite (substitution) rules that Marshall used to represent the pigeons' sexual behaviour. By application of the first rule, the overall *sexual*

1. Sexual behaviour sequence → Preparation + Consummation
2. Preparation → Introduction + Warm-up
   Introduction → Bowing (+Aggression)
   Aggression → $\left\{ \begin{array}{l} \text{(Driving +) Attacking} \\ \text{Driving (+ Attacking)} \end{array} \right\}$
   Warm-up → Displacement preening + Billing
   Consummation → Mounting + Copulating

*Figure 30*    Behaviour grammar for pigeon mating (from Hutt and Hutt 1970)

*behaviour sequence* can be rewritten as *preparation* plus *consummation*. *Preparation* can then be replaced by a more detailed specification of *introduction* plus *warm-up*, and so on. Figure 31 is a tree diagram showing one particular version of the behavioural organization which the rules in Figure 30 specify. The point to note is that there is no single fixed sequence of behaviour; many permutations of behaviour can occur in this situation. The task of the behaviour grammarian is to capture all and only the appropriate permutations in the most economical and accurate way. It is argued that grammatical notations, or something similar, can do this more efficiently than other types of statistical sequence models, for reasons we shall describe later.

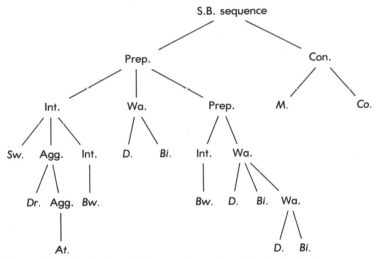

*Figure 31*   A behavioural 'sentence' produced by the behaviour grammar for pigeon mating (terminal items are in italics) (from Hutt and Hutt 1970)

We now turn to a few examples taken from the disciplines of artificial intelligence and computational linguistics. One view adopted in the analysis of language, as we have already seen, is that it is not sufficient to take a corpus of language and to extract organizing principles from it. It is also necessary to be able to do the reverse – that is, to state the generative principles clearly and rigorously enough that they can be turned into realistic examples of the language by systematic, and preferably mechanical, application. As the principles are very complex and have to be formulated within a network of interrelations, it is not always easy to determine what language a given set of principles would produce. One way of checking that the postulated principles really do produce the language in question is to build them into a computer program. This also forces one to state the principles clearly and completely explicitly. The program becomes a formalization and realization of the grammar, with which the computer can produce examples of sentences, or of arguments, stories, logical inferences, or any of the other things than can be represented by the extended notion of grammar. The realism, or lack of realism, of these products can then be used as a criterion for evaluating the program and for altering it where necessary.

One of the milestones in the computerized understanding of natural language was a program called SHRDLU, written by Terry Winograd. He was interested in the overall system of language, which not only produces sentences and recognizes meanings, but also is able to provide the appropriate sentences for a particular occasion, to act upon the sentences received, and so forth. A significant problem encountered in attempting this is the lack of autonomy of language. Language is not something that can be divorced from other forms of knowledge and from other forms of information processing. To have a completely functional language system you must also have a data base containing other kinds of knowledge outside the language itself, and a knowledge of the conventions of discourse. As a result Winograd had to build more than a simple language device; he also needed a 'universe of discourse' for the program. The universe of discourse in this case consisted of a 'block world', comprising geometrical figures, cubes, pyramids, cones and spheres, all of which could be represented on the computer's display screen. The computer 'knew' this world. It knew about certain properties of objects whereby, for instance, standing a pyramid on its base would be possible, but if it was put down on its point it would fall over. Likewise, putting a sphere on a slope would result in its rolling downwards. The program was also able to monitor where the objects were in relation to one another, and to act on the objects in response to commands, changing the state of the displayed world, and then 'converse' sensibly about the changes it had produced.

Here are a few short examples of the dialogues which ensued with SHRDLU. The first couplet is unproblematic: for the command 'Pick

A: Pick up the red block.
B: OK.

A: Grasp the pyramid.
B: I don't understand which pyramid you mean.

A: Find a block which is taller than
the one you are holding and put
it in the box.
B: By 'it' I assume you mean the block
which is taller than the one I am
holding.

*Figure 32* Talking to SHRDLU (from Winograd 1972)

up the red block', the machine answers 'OK' and the display shows the block being picked up. The command has been successfully interpreted and executed, and a social response in the form of language has been made. The second couplet, however, introduces ambiguity into the exchange. The operator's command was 'Grasp the pyramid'. There were two displayed pyramids on the computer's screen at this time, and the machine was unsure which pyramid to operate on. It responded 'I do not understand which pyramid you mean'. At this point the operator specified a particular pyramid, implicitly reinstating the original command without its original ambiguity, and the machine was able to carry out the task. Thirdly we have a slightly more complicated example of the computer's ability with dialogue. The command was 'Find a block which is taller than the one you are holding and put it in the box'. Although this may seem immediately comprehensible to us, the 'it' in the sentence is ambiguous, since there are a number of objects mentioned earlier in that same sentence. To be quite sure which object 'it' refers to, the computer came back with 'By "it" I assume you mean the block which is taller than the one I am holding'. When reassured on this point the machine went on to execute the command.

These exchanges may seem unremarkable and simple until you realize that most computers 'talk' FORTRAN, ALGOL, COBOL or some other 'high-level language', all of which are algebraic codes which have to be learnt by the programmer – whereas with Winograd's program the machine is able to respond in the native language of the programmer. This is important, both because it would be useful to have computers talking and understanding our own language, and because it may also help us understand more about the language itself. Writing natural-language programs forces us to specify theories in a way that reveals their properties and their faults. However, the drawback with this kind of work, and with Chomsky's conception of language described earlier, is the artificiality and simplicity of the phenomena they describe best. Some people claim that this severely limits the relevance and usefulness of such work for messier and less codifiable problems in the real world. It has even been suggested that this kind of research is a complete blind alley, and that a realistic understanding of real-world systems will not come from further and better models of the same kind, but from a different and less formalistic style of research. We would agree, although it has to be said that much of the most successful work in the natural sciences has depended on idealizations and simplifying assumptions of just as extreme a kind.

Natural-language programs, like all theories of language, have to relate form to meaning. Take a simple sentence like 'John killed his teacher.' When *we* see a sentence of this sort we are able to interpret it, and to infer its various implications, which enable us to answer questions such as 'Is John's teacher now dead?' or 'Was John's teacher alive before this incident?' or 'Was the teacher who has been killed John's teacher?' In other words this sentence seems to imply a number of other sentences in a way that is unproblematic for the human understanding process. In order for this sort of material to be *mechanically* processed, however, and its meaning extracted for use in making further inferences or answering questions, it is necessary that some kind of semantic representation is constructed out of each string of words, with the potential to support explicit inferences.

Consider the conceptual-dependency diagram in Figure 33. It shows the relationships between the various meaning elements in the example sentence, and how, at least in principle, a program would have to interpret the sentence in order to extract something approximating *our* understanding of its meaning. This 'essence' of meaning could then be used to deal with further enquiries or other operations relating to the sentence.

What the diagram shows is a basic transformation in $P$ (the past tense) of a *teacher* from the state *alive* to the state *dead*. The *teacher* is in the relation *possessed by* to *John*, and the transformation of the

John killed his teacher.

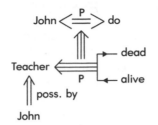

*Figure 33*    Conceptual-dependency diagram (from Schank 1973)

*teacher* from the state *alive* to the state *dead* in the *past* involved an action linked to *John*, who *did* something, also in the *past*. By systematically constructing this sort of diagram from the given sentences, and then scanning the diagram for information, one can in principle produce a system which is capable of answering a variety of additional questions about the original sentence, and in that sense construct a system which can understand natural language.

## Speech acts and social acts

According to the above view, language is principally a medium by which people send messages to one another, and its function is essentially to transfer statements or beliefs from one person to another. For many years language was viewed almost exclusively in these terms, and it seemed that it could be satisfactorily analysed by concentrating on its statement-making properties, and the truth or falsity of the statements made. The Oxford philosopher John Austin was one of the first to suggest that this kind of approach is very restricting. He believed that the idea of language as a message-sending system, measured according to the truth or falsity of its propositions, was only part of the story. The set of 'locutions' (all possible 'sayings') could, according to Austin, be separated into two distinct categories. The first category, which he called 'constative', consists of the propositional, message-sending utterances or state-ments – such as 'The carpet is brown' or 'The lights are on' or 'Today is Friday'. All of these constatives are capable of being either true or false on different occasions. The second class of locutions consisted of the 'performatives' or 'speech acts'. Performatives are not to do with truth or falsity, but rather are about 'How to do things with words', to use the title of Austin's famous book on the subject. They are utterances which use the medium of language to perform various social acts, such as a marriage ceremony, a christening, the launching of a ship, and so on. Such utterances are not concerned with truth or falsity but are performances, and often transformations, within the social world. Through this medium people commit themselves and others to obligations, make promises, blame and reprieve people, and so on, in each case with a socially defined significance.

While these social 'acts' cannot be true or false, they can either succeed or fail in other ways. Various relationships can exist between the formulation of a performative utterance and other aspects of the world, such as the speaker's circumstances, beliefs and observable actions. All these considerations can be prerequisites for the successful completion of a performative. Austin named the 'success' or 'failure' of performatives *felicity* and *infelicity* respectively – literally, 'happiness' or 'unhappiness' in the performance of a particular task.

At first the distinction between constative and performative utterances was to be made using an 'explicit performative formula'. This formula was invoked because not all performatives necessarily advertise that they *are* performatives. For instance, you do not always say 'I promise that . . .' or 'I predict that . . .' when you are making a promise or a prediction. Sometimes you just say 'I'll meet you later today' or 'Inflation will be 7 per cent next year'. These are respectively a promise and a prediction, though not explicitly labelled as such. Austin originally believed all performatives (and only they) *could* be prefixed by an explicit performative formula. In other words the message 'I shan't be late next time we meet' could equally well be rendered as '*I promise* I shan't be late next time we meet' and, according to Austin, the equivalence of the two utterances would indicate that we were dealing with a performative rather than a constative utterance, in both cases.

Unfortunately this simple formula for distinguishing performatives from constatives subsequently broke down. The boundary between the two categories is much more blurred than it seemed at first. Constatives can also take their own kind of explicit performative formula. If one is simply making a statement like 'The carpet is brown', one can equally well say 'I assert that the carpet is brown' or 'I declare that the carpet is brown'. It turns out that utterances

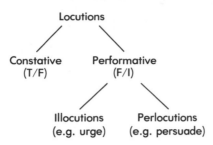

*Figure 34*  Things one can do with words

usually have both a constative and a performative aspect. Saying 'I promise that I will meet you under the clock at three' contains not only the performative formula 'I promise that . . .' but also a proposition 'I will meet you under the clock at three' which is capable of being true or false. The two categories are now usually seen as two sides of the same coin, and represented as F(p), for performative *force* and *propositional* content.

Another important distinction Austin made concerned two types of performatives called 'illocutions' and 'perlocutions'. Illocutions are social acts performed directly and necessarily *in* the saying of something. Perlocutions are performatives that *may* have certain social effects *as a result of* being said. The distinction may be clarified if we look at the difference between *urging* somebody to do something (an illocution) and *persuading* somebody to do something (a perlocution). The former is done merely by saying the appropriate words, but the latter requires more than that, and may or may not come about. If we say 'You really should read Smith's latest article; it contains a great deal of relevant material', then we have urged you to refer to that particular article. But whether we can be said to have *persuaded* you depends on many other factors besides our choice of words. You must take notice, remember, resolve to do it, and so on, all of which may or may not happen.

How many speech acts are there, and how important are they for social action? According to Austin there are over a thousand speech-act labels in the English vocabulary, which suggests they are very salient in our everyday conceptualizations. He classified them under the following five headings: (1) *verdictives*, which make some kind of judgement or professional assessment such as a diagnosis, acquittal or conviction; (2) *excercitives*, which make a free decision such as to appoint or dismiss an employee, or political voting; (3) *commissives*, which commit one with a promise, contract or covenant; (4) *behabitives*, which react to another's fortunes by offering, for instance, sympathy, apologies or thanks; and (5) *expositives*, which make statements, declarations, confirmations, and so on.

For the social scientist much of the significance of Austin's work lies not in its statements about language as such, but in the precedents it established for seeing social acts, whether performed in speech or not, in terms of their conventional function, and not merely their physical form. It has been one of the factors in the breaking of the stranglehold of behaviourism on psychological thinking, and it is no accident that Harré's central concept of 'acts', in his ethogenic view of social behaviour, resembles Austin's view of speech acts. Harré studied under Austin, as did John Searle, who has since continued and elaborated the philosophical tradition of speech-act theory.

Searle provides another useful classification of speech acts, and also a systematization of the criteria of classification. First, each speech act has a point or purpose, something it is supposed to do – for example, promising, asserting and predicting. Secondly, Searle introduced the notion of the 'direction of fit' between the world and the words, and thirdly he focused on the psychological states expressed by speech acts of different types. A command, statement or promise imply a wish, a belief or intention respectively, and this is one ground for considering them to be distinct classes of act. There are also many lesser differences which are involved in the classification of speech acts, such as the difference in *strength* between, for instance, suggesting and insisting; the difference in status of the speaker and hearer which distinguishes requesting from ordering; and differences in the interests of the speaker or hearer (in the sense of what is good or bad for them) which make the difference between a threat and a promise. Context (the relationship between the speech act and the rest of the discourse) and content can also affect the type of speech act. If I say 'It was raining yesterday' or 'It will be raining tomorrow', these similar sentences about the past and future become a report and a prediction respectively, but the difference lies in the propositional content and its time frame, rather than in any explicit performative construction.

Many but not all speech acts have counterparts which do not require speech. Things can be classified without the use of speech. Cards can be dealt into separate piles, or one can select particular

items by pointing to them. Some speech acts require special institutions to back them up, such as excommunicating someone, confer-
ring a degree, or naming a ship. Some can have explicit formulas,
whereas, rather interestingly, some speech acts go wrong if they are
given an explicit formula. For instance, if you said 'I hint that . . .',
somehow the very act of hinting would be changed by advertising the
fact that this was a hint. So it is not always the case that a speech act
can have an explicit formula. Sometimes such a formula would
destroy the very nature of the intended act. Lastly, there are stylistic
differences which differentiate speech-act types, such as the difference between announcing and confiding, which differ in tone of voice
rather than the choice of words.

1. Point or purpose of the type: its force.
2. Direction of fit.
3. Expressed psychological state.
4. Strength (suggest/insist).
5. Status/role of speaker/addressee.
6. Relation to interests of
   speaker/hearer (threaten/promise).
7. Relation with rest of discourse.
8. Propositional content (report/predict).
9. Necessarily *speech* act, cp. to classify.
10. External institution, e.g. to excommunicate.
11. Explicit formula available, cp. I hint, I boast.
12. Style: announcing/confiding.

*Figure 35* Criteria for speech-act classification

From Searle's three main features (function, direction of fit, and
implied psychological state) five principal classes of speech act can be
derived (see Figure 36). We need now to understand the idea of
'direction of fit'. To help with this we can use a visual mnemonic.
Imagine that language floats like a cloud of words above the surface
of the world. There are two possible directions of fit, represented by
arrows in Figure 36, pointing either downwards or upwards. When
the arrow points downwards from the words to the world, this means
that in that kind of speech act the words must be tailored to fit the events
in the world. When the arrow points upwards, the world is required
to correspond to the words. The five speech-act types picked out

| Force | | Direction of fit | ψ State |
|---|---|---|---|
| Representatives | ⊢ | ↓ | B(p) |
| Directives | ! | ↑ | W(H do A) |
| Commissives | C | ↑ | I(S do A) |
| Expressives | E | ∅ | (P) (S/H + prop.) |
| Declarations | D | ↕ | ∅ (p) |

*Figure 36*   Five types of speech act

by Searle's criteria are *representatives, directives, commissives, expressives* and *declarations*. We shall describe each class in turn.

A *representative* is a factual use of language, rather like the old 'constative' in Austin's scheme. The onus of correspondence lies with the words to fit with the world. The implied psychological state is *belief* in a *proposition* B(p). In the case of *directives* the implied logical formula is slightly different. Directives can be loosely defined as 'commands', and the direction of fit is from the world to the words. That is, the world must adapt to what is said. The correspondence between a command and a state of affairs in the world is achieved because somebody adjusts their behaviour in accordance with the command. The implied psychological state is a *wish* (W) on the part of the speaker that the *hearer acts* in a certain way, for which the formula is W(H do A). Thirdly, the *commissive* (or 'promise') also has a direction of fit from world to words, but here it is the speaker's actions, not the hearer's, which must fit in with the words. The implied psychological state is *intention* (I) that the *speaker* do some *action* (A). The formula is therefore I(S do A). Fourthly, an *expressive* would be something like 'I hope you'll soon be feeling better' or 'I hope that my cough will go if I drink some water'. There is no direction of fit, so instead of arrows the figure shows the null symbol ∅. The *psychological state* (P) can stand for hopes, wishes, fears, regrets, apologies, and so on, and is expressed about some property of either the speaker or the hearer. Finally, in a *declaration*, you 'declare' something to be so, like the opening of parliament or the closing of a factory. This kind of act has the rather interesting property that the direction of fit goes up and down, from world to words and from words to world. For instance, when one says 'I now declare this bridge is open', one is both describing a state of affairs, and bringing about the state of affairs which is described.

## Semiotics

At the turn of this century the linguist Ferdinand de Saussure was doing pioneering work on the structure of language and other systems of signs which has given many concepts to the study of action systems. Among his original contributions was the explication of four rather important dichotomies, the first of which we have already met – between 'diachronic' and 'synchronic' structures. These terms were originally used to contrast the study of the way in which language changes over the generations and centuries, and the study of a language as it is now, or at some other given time. This is rather like the distinction between a moving picture and a still photograph. The way the terms diachronic and synchronic are used nowadays has been adapted to refer to any temporally structured or long-term phenomena or, on the other hand, any instantaneous phenomena. The second distinction drawn by Saussure was between *la langue* and *la parole*. *Langue* is the abstract system of language 'out there' in the world, in its broadest sense, such as the French language, the English language, the Chinese language, and so on. *Parole*, by contrast, is the concrete product – the written or spoken messages as they are observed. Thirdly, Saussure formulated the distinction between 'syntagmatic' and 'paradigmatic' structures. The syntagmatic structure is the set of relations between elements of a language, according to which they combine into larger constructions such as sentences. Paradigmatic relationships between elements of language are those which show them to be similar, synonymous, dissimilar, antithetical, and so on. This dichotomy was introduced earlier, in the discussion of behavioural meaning. Finally there was a dichotomy between 'signifier' and 'signified'.

**Saussure's principal dichotomies for describing the structure of language**

| | |
|---|---|
| synchronic | diachronic |
| *langue* | *parole* |
| syntagmatic | paradigmatic (formerly associative) |
| signifier (acoustic image) | signified (concept) |

Saussure's programme also included the idea that language is just one part of a general system of signs. It was he who coined the term 'semiology' for the study of sign systems of all kinds, whether realized in dance, talk, writing, abstract symbols, gestures, and so forth. Semiology deals with the relations between signifiers and their meanings, which are sometimes divided into the following three types. The first type is called an *icon*, which is a sign that represents something else by virtue of its resemblance. Thus a photograph may be a sign for a person because the photograph and the person resemble one another; no additional convention is needed to understand the icon. Secondly, an *index* is a sign related to its object by cause and effect. A knock on the door means someone is present, although the event does not resemble the person. Finally the most important type of sign is the *symbol*, where the relation between sign and object is arbitrary, and culturally determined. For example, a word like 'tree' is an arbitrary collection of sounds or marks, which represents a tree only by virtue of associations that speakers of English have learned.

## Breaking the code

The real point of this chapter is to consider not linguistic analyses of language, but linguistic (and similar) analyses of things which are not language. We can use linguistic frameworks to look at a range of combinatorial studies of event sequences, because linguistic analysis is also largely concerned with the characterization of its subject matter as a sequence of classifiable units or events. In the case of an ordinary grammar for a language, the units would be morphemes and the sequences would be the sentences of the language. The grammar would be used by the linguist to specify how the morphemes 'fit together' over time into diachronic patterns and constructions, but the tools for doing that kind of investigation are not needed only by people studying language. Similar techniques have also been developed in the other disciplines which need to examine the organization of events over time. In many cases these alternative methods are statistical techniques, but they share many similarities with the conceptions used in writing and evaluating a grammar. Most of the methods we shall be describing have been borrowed from animal ethology, and were originally used to 'decode' animal behavioural sequences.

Figure 37 shows something resembling a 'snake', representing a

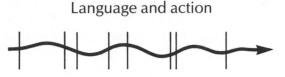

*Figure 37*    Parsing the course of events

course of events unfolding over time. The string of events to be analysed could be almost anything: an argument, a dialogue, a relationship, a biography or, for that matter, a sentence. All these things share a common denominator. They occur as an orderly progression of events through time, which we have represented diagrammatically as a meandering line running from left to right. The vertical lines are the boundaries between different events. The aim is to turn a family of complex sequences of events into an economic picture of the structuring principles of the system which underlie the *set* of *possible* sequences.

This can be achieved by following a three-step procedure of 'unitizing', 'classifying' and 'sequence analysis'. (Sometimes 'unitizing' is called 'parsing' or 'segmentation', and 'classifying' can be called 'taxonomy' or 'categorization'.) In order to make sense of the series of events we first have to be able to find the boundaries *between* each successive event − which is the unitizing stage − although this does not as yet *identify* the separate events. A number of methods of unitizing have been suggested, but the details do not matter here. They all work by judging where the greatest discontinuities of form or function lie within the behaviour stream, sometimes by combining the views of a number of judges into a single consensual picture.

In the second or classifying stage, we need to put events into category schemes or type classes, which are often given arbitrary labels, such as letters of the alphabet. But how does one decide which are the *right* classes to impose on a complex pattern of events over time? If we take face-value classifications, such as the apparent meaning of events, we may well end up with categories that are unsuitable for sequence analysis. For the specific purpose of sequence analysis, all the events sharing the same *combinatorial* properties must be allocated to the same class. Any two events which have different rules of combination with the other events must be put into different classes. All other principles of classification will be inconsistent with the demands of subsequent sequence analysis. A principle adopted for just this reason by linguists and some early chemists can be used to produce the appropriate type of classification. It is known as the substitution (or commutation) procedure. As the name of the procedure suggests, it classifies individual items or events on the basis of their substitutability within larger structures. As we saw earlier, this was the original basis of Mendeleev's periodic table of the chemical elements, and the same kind of reasoning also underlies many of the standard syntactic categorizations used in linguistics. The elements which belong in a single class can all be substituted for one another without disrupting the overall structure in which they fit, be that a sentence, a molecule or a life story. This implies that they all share the same 'valency', the same sort of combinatorial properties or rules of combination.

To carry out the substitution procedure by inspection, without further specialized procedures being used, one requires simple material that lends itself to an easy interpretation of the elements being classified. However, this is not usually the case, and more complex material may defy unaided classification, so we usually need quantitative techniques to help in the classification task. Even then the precision of the resulting classification may be more apparent than real. Categories which really have rather 'blurred' edges, and which blend into each other with numerous borderline cases, may come out looking misleadingly clear and distinctive. It is rather as if things that really occur in 'fuzzy sets', and can be members of various sets to different extents measured on a scale from 0 to 1, had been described in terms of classical set theory, where everything is completely in or out of each set, and even may be restricted to membership of only one set at a time.

The transitional-frequency matrix, which was introduced in Chapter 1, is the usual starting-point for the quantitative reclassification of events. In Figure 38 the letters $i$ and $j$ stand for two distinct behavioural types as identified in a preliminary analysis, and which recur in different sequential combinations with other events. This matrix serves as a record of the entire sequence of events by showing the number of times event type $i$ was followed by event type $j$; the number of times event type $j$ was followed by event type $i$; and so on. What we are aiming for is a measure of how similar the events $i$ and $j$ are to one another, in the specific sense of how appropriately they would substitute for one another in a variety of contexts. This can be determined by finding out which things most (or least) commonly follow (or precede) $i$ and $j$, and so on for all other event-type pairs. By

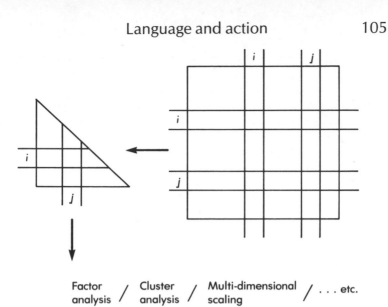

Factor / Cluster / Multi-dimensional / ... etc.
analysis / analysis / scaling

*Figure 38* The transitional-frequency matrix as a basis for event classification

working down the values in columns *i* and *j* we can see the similarities in the events which normally *precede i* and *j*, while their respective rows show which events commonly *follow i* and *j*. If a high correlation is found between the two rows and the two columns relating to *i* and *j*, this means that *i* and *j* are substitutable, because they tend to share the same antecedents and the same sequiturs. A corresponding correlation coefficient has to be determined for every possible pair of types from the preliminary classification. To the extent that two types of events correlate, they should be combined. To the extent that they do not correlate, or correlate inversely, they should be kept as separate categories. The correlations are then arranged as a similarity matrix (see Figure 38). The similarity matrix is a triangular half-matrix, as described in Chapter 1, which forms the basis for factor analysis, cluster analysis or multidimensional scaling of items to produce the final system of revised categories. Now, having produced a numerical taxonomy of events, we can move on to the sequence analysis itself.

The transitional-frequency matrix has serious limitations as a final picture of the sequence patterns themselves. The kind of inferences that common sense would suggest can be drawn from it are often quite invalid. The matrix may show that event *i* is frequently followed by event $j$, and also that event $j$ is frequently followed by event $k$. But it would be incorrect to conclude that a large number of $i$–$j$–$k$ triplets could be found in the data. To take a concrete example using the '$i$ before $e$ except after $c$' spelling rule in English, you would find $i$ followed by $e$, and $c$ followed by $i$, as high-probability pairs within a matrix drawn up from letters in English text, but the corresponding triplet $c$–$i$–$e$, which would seem to be implied by this, would be completely absent from the data (except in the plurals of words whose singular ends in $cy$, such as tendencies). It is impossible to turn the pairwise relations given by the matrix into a comprehensive picture of the overall constructions within a string, because the pairwise relations are intransitive. One way of achieving a more comprehensive analysis of longer behavioural chains is to build up a more elaborate 'higher-order' matrix. Instead of relating each item to just the preceding item, a second-order matrix may be used. This shows the probability of every possible third event following every possible combination of two preceding events. The second-order matrix might sound quite straightforward, but in fact it opens up a range of further difficulties. Instead of simply relating items to individual antecedents like $i$, $j$ or $k$, a second-order matrix has to relate each possible sequitur to the prior occurrence of $ii$, $ij$, $ik$ . . . and then $ji$, $jj$, $jk$ . . . and so on. The problem gets rapidly worse with even higher order matrices. To find anything interesting about a behaviour sequence like a conversation, you would probably need to examine about fifty types of event, each considered in relation to five or so previous events, producing a matrix with 15,625,000,000 cells. Clearly this is not a feasible strategy to adopt. In addition to the problem of higher orders of pattern, a sequence analysis of this kind must satisfy two further criteria if its validity is not to be questionable. The sequential patterns being studied must be stationary, that is their transitional probabilities must be constant; and they must be homogeneous, that is not consisting of a mixed sample from different systems with different rules and regularities of sequential organization.

The system of chain analysis devised by Richard Dawkins in Oxford provides a neat method for making higher-order inferences about sequences without constructing enormous $n^{\text{th}}$ order matrices. A computer program is used to seek out the most probable event pairs in a given transitional-probability matrix. Suppose that the most common transition existed between event $i$ and event $j$. In this procedure a new row and column would then be added to the outside of the matrix to accommodate the transitions to and from the *ij* pair. The computer scans the matrix and revises the values *i* and *j* when they occur unpaired. In the same way the procedure then seeks out the second most common pair, which might be *ij* followed by *i*. Again, a new row and column would be drawn up to accommodate the *iji* triplet, and previous values adjusted in the body of the matrix. This procedure is repeated until it has built up a picture of all the recurring chains of events in the data, in descending order of frequency of occurrence. Each time the procedure is repeated, it need only add one more row and column to the matrix. Valid inferences may be drawn about long behaviour chains using this technique, without the need for cumbersome higher-order matrices.

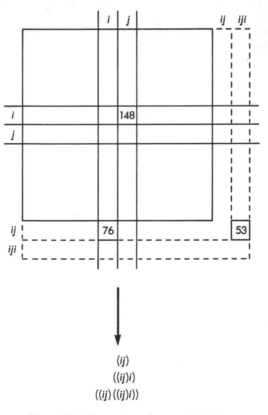

*Figure 39*   Detection of extended chains

The next problem we encounter with sequence analysis is that the structures are not usually confined to a single level of description. The behaviour chains are not like beads on a string, where the structure is completely captured by their order of succession. There are *hierarchical* structures which organize the behavioural pattern on several different levels of description. This can be studied by dividing the transitional-probability (or transitional-frequency) matrix into gross regions representing the postulated higher-order units of activity, which might be called A, B and C, as in Figure 40. If all the behavioural units subsumed under A are extremely closely connected, and really do make up a distinct behavioural mode or higher-order unit, and likewise for B and C, then the internal relations of these super-groups – that is to say the pattern of A-type units leading to other A-type units, or Bs to Bs, or Cs to Cs – will be clearly marked. The super-cells in that matrix will therefore all have high $\chi^2$ values. In other words, there will be systematic sequential relations between antecedents and sequiturs *within* any of the three behavioural modes, but between items from *different* behavioural modes low $\chi^2$ values would be expected. If the behavioural modes have been inappropriately defined, a further computer program can be used to trade individual rows and columns between the gross classes until $\chi^2$ values on the leading diagonal cells are maximized. This indicates that the best characterization of super- and sub-groups of behaviour has been reached, within the limits of this technique.

There are other ways of dealing statistically with sequences of

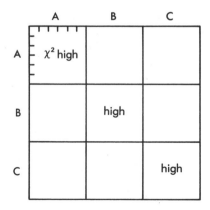

*Figure 40*   Detection of hierarchical organization

events, which use quite different ideas from those of the above procedures. Some do not deal with events in terms of their antecedents and sequiturs, but rather they examine them according to the distribution of real-time intervals between successive events. Either the events can be of the same class, or else the beginning and ending of each interval of time can be marked by two different classes of events. Such methods allow the examination of 'action at a distance' or causal influences between events well separated in time. The time intervals can be indefinitely long, so the method could be used in principle to study the effect of events in childhood on behaviour in later life, for example.

A simple example involving a single category of event is represented in Figure 41. Time runs from left to right, and the single type of event recurring over time is shown as a distribution of vertical lines. We want to find out if the temporal distribution of these events is random or non-random, or to put it another way, whether the probability of one of these events occurring in a given interval of time is influenced systematically by the length of time since it last occurred. If its probability of happening in any given sampling interval is always the same, *regardless* of the time which has elapsed since it last occurred, then the sequence is a random distribution of events, in the sense of this analysis. If, on the other hand, recent occurrences of the event make it more or less likely to happen again, then the occurrence of the events has a non-random organization.

The procedure was originally devised to deal with ecological issues, particularly the analysis of life-span data, and it can be most easily understood in those terms. Think of the marked events on Figure 41 as separating a population of time intervals between the birth and death of a number of individual organisms. These data can be replotted as a 'survivor function' – the proportion of individuals (or time intervals) surviving plotted against age, as in Figure 42. Since mortality is a one-way process, obviously as age *increases* the proportion of survivors *decreases*. This is what is called a monotonic

*Figure 41*   Time-interval analysis

function, because it can only ever have one 'tone' or gradient, in this case downwards. The steepness of the gradient can vary, but the direction cannot. At most it can enter a horizontal plateau, called a point of inflection, before continuing on downwards. The key question is whether the chances of an individual dying in any given year *increase* as the individual grows older. Or is the likelihood of death unrelated to age, for some parts of the life-course at least? If the latter is the case, the survivor function exhibits a peculiar characteristic. Suppose that, during any single observation period, the probability of an organism dying was 50 per cent, or in the case of the more general time-interval analysis, the chance of the next event occurring, and thus 'killing' the time interval, was always 50 per cent, regardless of how long that time interval was. Then we would find that, between time of observation *zero* and time *one*, half of the population had died (or in the case of time-interval analysis, half of the time intervals had finished with the next occurrence of the event in question). Between time *one* and time *two*, 50 per cent of the remaining half would die, leaving a quarter. Between times *two* and *three* another half of the remaining quarter would go, leaving an eighth, and so on. If the probability remained fixed, the decline in numbers in the population would be exponential. If the ordinate of the graph, showing the proportion of the population surviving, had been plotted on a logarithmic scale, the result would be not a survivor function, but a *log*-survivor function, and what would have been an exponential curve would show up as a straight line. The presence of a straight line in a log-survivor plot clearly identifies the random spacing of events.

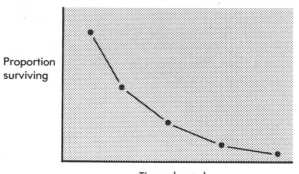

*Figure 42*   Survivor function

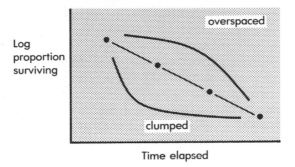

*Figure 43*    Log-survivor function

When events are 'clumped' (that is, when short time intervals are more common than in the random case, as when organisms die young rather than old), the curve bends towards the origin. On the other hand, when the events are 'overspaced' (indicating a high incidence of long time intervals, or, in the case of animals, that they do well when young but have a high mortality in old age), the curve bends away from the origin. In real behaviour patterns there are often alternating periods of clumping and overspacing, which produce a characteristic 'signature' on the log-survivor plot, shown in Figure 44. This unique signature enables us to distinguish the 'bout and space' behaviour pattern from others, to say something about the processes governing it, and to describe the length of the periods of

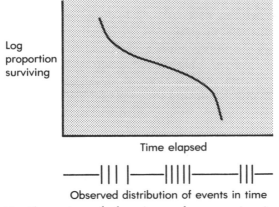

*Figure 44*   Alternation of clumping and overspacing in log-survivor function

satiation and activity which make it up. All in all, this is a rather different approach to the analysis of sequences of events from the study of transitions between successive types.

Finally, an interesting control-theory conception of behaviour was suggested by Miller, Galanter and Pribram as part of one of the early attempts to use generative linguistic notions to describe action structure. Called the 'Test Operate Test Exit' routine (or TOTE), it is a simple cybernetic mechanism which is capable of monitoring the performance of a task, repeating the requisite operations until monitoring shows a satisfactory state of affairs, and then stopping. Let us consider the simple case of a set of rules that would form a TOTE routine for hammering in a nail. If the instructions said 'Hit the head of the nail ten times' they would be inadequate, because depending on various factors, such as the force of the hammering and the density of the wood, the nail might go home on the first blow, or still be sticking out from the wood after the tenth. A better set of instructions would be sensitive to the changing state of the world. The TOTE format provides such a routine in the form of a negative-feedback loop. In the case of the nail, the TOTE controller would hit the nail and then monitor the position of the nail in relation to the wood. If the nail did not lie flush with the wood (the negative condition), then the procedure would revert to the 'operate' mode and hammer the nail one more time. The procedure would continue in this way until monitoring revealed a positive condition – that is, the nail lying flush with the wood. At this point it would exit from the routine, with the task accomplished.

These routines can be combined to form complex behaviour-simulating cybernetic programs, by the chaining together and nesting of super- and sub-procedures. The point of this is to create a complete and coherent 'map' of the action system in question, in which the properties and functions of all the parts can be seen in relation to the constitution and structure of the whole, instead of the easier but entirely unsatisfactory kind of analysis, where each part of a complex system is taken and studied in isolation from the rest. Furthermore these 'maps' are dynamic, moving, growing, evolving, reacting representations, which do not merely store the same facts and the same events for all time, but have behavioural properties of their own, which mimic those of the system they represent. For this reason they can be used for learning, experimenting and trying out new skills and procedures, in the way that fragmentary or static images cannot. These considerations bring us to the matter of self-controlling mechanisms, cybernetics and computer models of behaviour, which we discuss in the next chapter.

## Further reading

Altman, S. A. (1965) 'Sociobiology of Rhesus Monkeys II: stochastics of social communication'. *Journal of Theoretical Biology*, 8, 490–522.

Attneave, F. (1959) *Applications of Information Theory to Psychology: A Summary of Basic Concepts, Methods and Results*. London: Holt, Rinehart & Winston.

Austin, J. L. (1962) *How to do Things with Words*. Oxford: Clarendon.

Bakeman, R. (1978) 'Untangling streams of behaviour: sequential analyses of observation data'. In G. P. Sackett (ed.), *Observing Behaviour*, Vol. 2: *Data Collection and Analysis Methods*. Baltimore, Md: University Park Press.

Bandler, R., and Grinder, J. (1975) *The Structure of Magic: A Book about Language and Therapy*. Palo Alto, Cal.: Science and Behavior Books.

Campbell, J. (1983) *Grammatical Man: Information, Entropy, Language and Life*. London: Allen Lane.

Chatfield, C. (1977) 'Some recent developments in time-series analysis'. *Journal of the Royal Statistical Society*, 140 (4), 492–510.

Chomsky, N. (1965) *Aspects of the Theory of Syntax*. The Hague: Mouton.

Chomsky, N. (1968) *Language and Mind*. New York: Harcourt Brace Jovanovich.

Chomsky, N. (1980) *Rules and Representations*. Oxford: Blackwell.

Collett, P., and Lamb, R. (1982) 'Describing sequences of social interaction'. In M. von Cranach and R. Harré (eds), *The Analysis of Action*. Cambridge: Cambridge University Press.

Coulthart, M. (1977) *An Introduction to Discourse Analysis*. London: Longman.

Culler, J. (1978) *Saussure*. Glasgow: Fontana.

Dawkins, R. (1976) 'Hierarchical organisation: a candidate principle for ethology'. In P. P. G. Bateson and R. A. Hinde (eds), *Growing Points in Ethology*. Cambridge: Cambridge University Press.

Farb, P. (1974) *Wordplay: What Happens when People Talk*. London: Cape.

Foa, U. G., and Turner, J. L. (1970) 'Psychology in the year 2000: going structural?' *American Psychologist*, 25, 244–7.

Hertel, R. K. (1972) 'Application of stochastic process analyses to the study of psychotherapeutic processes'. *Psychological Bulletin*, 77, 421–30.

Hewes, D. E. (1979) 'The sequential analysis of social interaction'. *Quarterly Journal of Speech*, 65, 56–73.

Holtzman, W. H. (1962) 'Statistical models for the study of change in single cases'. In C. W. Harris (ed.), *Problems in Measuring Change*. Madison, Wisc.: University of Wisconsin Press.

Hutt, S. J., and Hutt, C. (1970) *Direct Observation and Measurement of Behaviour*. Springfield, Ill.: Thomas.

Kemeny, J. G., and Snell, J. L. (1960) *Finite Markov Chains*. Princeton, NJ: Van Nostrand.

Knoke, D., and Burke, P. J. (1980) *Log Linear Models. Quantitative Applications in the Social Sciences*, no. 20. Beverly Hills, Cal.: Sage.

Labov, W., and Fansell, D. (1977) *Therapeutic Discourse*. New York: Academic Press.

Lashley, K. S. (1951) 'The problem of serial order in behaviour'. In L. A. Jeffress (ed.), *Cerebral Mechanisms in Behaviour*. New York: Wiley.

Lyons, J. (1970) *Chomsky*. London: Fontana.

Melbin, M. (1972) *Alone with Others*. New York: Harper & Row.

Miller, G. A. (1967) *The Psychology of Communication*. New York: Basic Books.

Miller, G., Galanter, E., and Pribram, K. (1960) *Plans and the Structure of Behaviour*. New York: Holt, Rinehart & Winston.

Mischel, W. (1977) 'On the future of personality measurement'. *American Psychologist*, 32 (4), 246–54.

Pörn, I. (1977) *Action Theory and Social Science: Some Formal Models*. Boston, Mass.: Reidel.

Rausch, H. L. (1972) 'Process and change: a Markovian model for interaction'. *Family Process*, 11, 275–98.

Rawls, J. (1955) 'Two concepts of rules'. *Philosophical Review*, 64, 3–32.

Robey, D. (ed.) (1973) *Structuralism*. Oxford: Clarendon.

Runyan, W. M. (1980) 'A stage-state analysis of the life course'. *Journal of Personality and Social Psychology*, 38 (6), 951–62.

Saussure, F. de (1974) *Course in General Linguistics*. Trans. Wade Baskin. London: Fontana.

Schank, R. C. (1973) 'Identification of conceptualizations underlying natural language'. In R. C. Schank and K. M. Colby (eds), *Computer Models of Thought and Language*. San Francisco, Cal.: Freeman.

Searle, J. (1969) *Speech Acts*. Cambridge: Cambridge University Press.

Searle, J. (1975) 'A taxonomy of illocutionary acts'. In K. Gunderson (ed.), *Language, Mind and Knowledge*. Minnesota Studies in Philosophy of Science, 7, Minneapolis, Minn., University of Minnesota Press.

Segal, E. M., and Stacy, E. W., Jr (1975) 'Rule governed behaviour as a psychological process'. *American Psychologist*, 30, 541–52.

Shannon, C. E. (1948) 'A mathematical theory of communication'. *Bell System Technical Journal*, 27, 379–423.

Slater, P. J. B. (1973) 'Describing sequences of behaviour'. In P. P. G. Bateson and P. H. Klopfer (eds), *Perspectives in Ethology*. New York: Plenum.

Thorndyke, P. W. (1977) 'Cognitive structures in comprehension and memory of narrative discourse'. *Cognitive Psychology*, 9, 77–110.

Van Der Kloot, W., and Morse, M. J. (1975) 'A stochastic analysis of the display behaviour of the red-breasted merganser (Mergus serrator)'. *Behaviour*, 54, 181–216.

Van Hooff, J. A. R. A. M. (1973) 'A structural analysis of the social behaviour of a semi-captive group of chimpanzees'. In M. von Cranach and I. Vine (eds), *Social Communication and Movement*. London: Academic Press.

Winograd, T. (1972) *Understanding Natural Language*. Edinburgh: Edinburgh University Press.

# 4

# Systems and cybernetics

## Analysis and synthesis: the concept of a 'system'

If you have ever tried to communicate in a foreign language armed only with a phrasebook, you will know the feelings of frustration and inadequacy when you finally realize that a catalogue of pieces is not a substitute for an understanding of the language as a whole. In this chapter we shall turn to the central issues surrounding the idea of synthesis as opposed to analysis, to consider how the elements of behavioural systems can be integrated into a coherent framework which reveals the 'emergent properties' of the whole. These are the properties which are produced by the overall system in a way that seems to transcend the limitations of the component parts.

Let us first examine a concrete example of the way a holistic approach can be used in the study of animal behaviour. Figure 45 shows a behaviour grammar for the flight patterns of a foraging honey bee, produced by Ronald Westman. This representation of the complex configurations of behaviour can capture things which a conventional statistical analysis of behaviour sequences cannot, and furthermore can capture them in a very economical formulation. This is important not only for the student of bee behaviour, who prefers economy and brevity, but also for the bee, which must package its behavioural strategies as efficiently as possible into a small mass of nerve tissue, so that it can fly about with the minimum

$$G_4 = \langle V_T, V_N, P, B \rangle$$

where $V_T = \{r_{135}, r_{90}, r_{45}, s, l_{45}, l_{90}, l_{135}, d_1, d_5, d_{20}, h\}$

where $d_X$ means fly x metres, and h means 'go home'.

$V_N = \{B, M_1, M_2, M_3, M_4\}$, and P is the following set of productions:

| | | | |
|---|---|---|---|
| 1) | $B \rightarrow M_1 M_2$ | $\{2(.4), 3(.3), 4(.3)\}$ | $\{\emptyset\}$ |
| 2) | $M_1 \rightarrow r_{45} d_{20}$ | $\{5(R=1), 10(R=0)\}$ | $\{\emptyset\}$ |
| 3) | $M_1 \rightarrow s d_{20}$ | $\{5(R=1), 10(R=0)\}$ | $\{\emptyset\}$ |
| 4) | $M_1 \rightarrow l_{45} d_{20}$ | $\{5(R=1), 10(R=0)\}$ | $\{\emptyset\}$ |
| 5) | $M_2 \rightarrow M_2 M_3$ | $\{6(.25), 7(.25), 8(.25), 9(.25)\}$ | $\{\emptyset\}$ |
| 6) | $M_2 \rightarrow r_{90} d_1$ | $\{14(R=1), 19(R=0)\}$ | $\{\emptyset\}$ |
| 7) | $M_2 \rightarrow r_{45} d_1$ | $\{14(R=1), 19(R=0)\}$ | $\{\emptyset\}$ |
| 8) | $M_2 \rightarrow l_{45} d_1$ | $\{14(R=1), 19(R=0)\}$ | $\{\emptyset\}$ |
| 9) | $M_2 \rightarrow l_{90} d_1$ | $\{14(R=1), 19(R=0)\}$ | $\{\emptyset\}$ |
| 10) | $M_2 \rightarrow M_2 M_3$ | $\{11(.4), 12(.3), 13(.3)\}$ | $\{\emptyset\}$ |
| 11) | $M_2 \rightarrow r_{45} d_5$ | $\{25(R=1), 31(R=0)\}$ | $\{\emptyset\}$ |
| 12) | $M_2 \rightarrow s d_5$ | $\{25(R=1), 31(R=0)\}$ | $\{\emptyset\}$ |
| 13) | $M_2 \rightarrow l_{45} d_5$ | $\{25(R=1), 31(R=0)\}$ | $\{\emptyset\}$ |
| 14) | $M_3 \rightarrow M_4 M_3$ | $\{37 \text{ if } \Sigma R > 50;\ 15(.3), 16(.2), 17(.2), 18(.3)\}$ | $\{\emptyset\}$ |
| 15) | $M_4 \rightarrow r_{135} d_1$ | $\{14(R=1), 19(R=0)\}$ | $\{\emptyset\}$ |
| 16) | $M_4 \rightarrow r_{90} d_1$ | $\{14(R=1), 19(R=0)\}$ | $\{\emptyset\}$ |
| 17) | $M_4 \rightarrow l_{90} d_1$ | $\{14(R=1), 19(R=0)\}$ | $\{\emptyset\}$ |
| 18) | $M_4 \rightarrow l_{135} d_1$ | $\{14(R=1), 19(R=0)\}$ | $\{\emptyset\}$ |
| 19) | $M_3 \rightarrow M_3 M_4$ | $\{37 \text{ if } \Sigma R > 50;\ 20(.2), 21(.2), 22(.2), 23(.2), 24(.2)\}$ | $\{\emptyset\}$ |
| 20) | $M_3 \rightarrow r_{90} d_5$ | $\{25(R=1), 31(R=0)\}$ | $\{\emptyset\}$ |
| 21) | $M_3 \rightarrow r_{45} d_5$ | $\{25(R=1), 31(R=0)\}$ | $\{\emptyset\}$ |
| 22) | $M_3 \rightarrow s d_5$ | $\{25(R=1), 31(R=0)\}$ | $\{\emptyset\}$ |
| 23) | $M_3 \rightarrow l_{45} d_5$ | $\{25(R=1), 31(R=0)\}$ | $\{\emptyset\}$ |
| 24) | $M_3 \rightarrow l_{90} d_5$ | $\{25(R=1), 31(R=0)\}$ | $\{\emptyset\}$ |
| 25) | $M_3 \rightarrow M_3 M_4$ | $\{37 \text{ if } \Sigma R > 50;\ 26(.3), 27(.15), 28(.1), 29(.15), 30(.3)\}$ | $\{\emptyset\}$ |
| 26) | $M_3 \rightarrow r_{90} d_1$ | $\{14(R=1), 19(R=0)\}$ | $\{\emptyset\}$ |
| 27) | $M_3 \rightarrow r_{45} d_1$ | $\{14(R=1), 19(R=0)\}$ | $\{\emptyset\}$ |
| 28) | $M_3 \rightarrow s d_1$ | $\{14(R=1), 19(R=0)\}$ | $\{\emptyset\}$ |
| 29) | $M_3 \rightarrow l_{45} d_1$ | $\{14(R=1), 19(R=0)\}$ | $\{\emptyset\}$ |
| 30) | $M_3 \rightarrow l_{90} d_1$ | $\{14(R=1), 19(R=0)\}$ | $\{\emptyset\}$ |
| 31) | $M_3 \rightarrow M_3 M_4$ | $\{37 \text{ if } \Sigma F > 150;\ 32(.2), 33(.2), 34(.2), 35(.2), 36(.2)\}$ | $\{\emptyset\}$ |
| 32) | $M_3 \rightarrow r_{90} d_{20}$ | $\{25(R=1), 31(R=0)\}$ | $\{\emptyset\}$ |
| 33) | $M_3 \rightarrow r_{45} d_{20}$ | $\{25(R=1), 31(R=0)\}$ | $\{\emptyset\}$ |
| 34) | $M_3 \rightarrow s d_{20}$ | $\{25(R=1), 31(R=0)\}$ | $\{\emptyset\}$ |
| 35) | $M_3 \rightarrow l_{45} d_{20}$ | $\{25(R=1), 31(R=0)\}$ | $\{\emptyset\}$ |
| 36) | $M_3 \rightarrow l_{90} d_{20}$ | $\{25(R=1), 31(R=0)\}$ | $\{\emptyset\}$ |
| 37) | $M_4 \rightarrow h$ | $\{\emptyset\}$ | |

*Figure 45* Behaviour grammar for honey bee foraging (from Westman 1977)

waste of energy and the greatest possible spare capacity for its 'payload'.

There are four parts to the grammar: a terminal vocabulary, a non-terminal vocabulary, a set of productions, and the symbol B for the behaviour to be represented – very much as the sentence grammar in Chapter 3 consisted of $V_T$, $V_N$, P and S. The terminal vocabulary consists of behavioural symbols depicting what the bee actually *does*. The non-terminal vocabulary is a set of algebraical symbols which are used in the derivation of the final behaviour, but which do not appear in the eventual behavioural description. Thirdly, the set of productions (the rules of the grammar) are similar to the rewrite rules used in classical sentence grammars. Finally, the B symbol is used just like S in a sentence grammar, and is the overall representation of the string prior to elaboration.

The grammar shows that the behaviour chains of the foraging bee break down into two components $M_1$ and $M_2$, which in turn break down in various alternative ways, as specified by further grammatical rules. The terminal vocabulary is fairly self-explanatory: for example, '$r_{90}d_1$' means that the bee turns $90°$ to the *right* and flies ahead a *distance* of *one* metre. In addition to standard notational devices that might be found in most rewrite-rule grammars for language, there are some less orthodox features in Westman's system. The expression in curly brackets to the right of each rule specifies the conditions according to which the grammar chooses its next option from each of the possible rules. $\{14(R=1), 19(R=0)\}$ means that if food is found at this stage $(R=1)$ the grammar goes next to line 14, otherwise it goes to line 19. In this respect the grammar's format is rather like a 'production system', a list of circumstance–action pairs, to be taken in order.

Let us work through an example. The grammar starts in state B for the general description of the sequence of behaviour to be elaborated. Application of rule 1 gives us $M_1M_2$ and the options of going to rules 2, 3 or 4 with probabilities of 0.4, 0.3 and 0.3 respectively. If a weighted random selection were to send us next to rule 2, we should then have $r_{45}d_{20}$, $M_2$ by replacement of $M_1$. Suppose the bee finds food at this point. The condition $\{5(R = 1), 10(R = 0)\}$ in rule 2 would next send us to rule 5: $M_2 \rightarrow M_2M_3$. So now the string would read $r_{45}d_{20}$, $M_2$, $M_3$, and another weighted random choice leading, say, to rule 9. Rule 9 then converts the string to $r_{45}d_{20}$, $l_{90}d_1$, $M_3$. If there is no find here $\{. . . 19(R = 0)\}$, the grammar moves to rule 19.

The string now reads $r_{45}d_{20}$, $l_{90}d_1$, $M_3$, $M_4$. And so the search pattern continues. After 50 finds, the condition $\{37 \text{ if } \Sigma R \geqslant 50 \ldots\}$ in rules 14, 19, or 25 sends the grammar to rule 37, $M_4 \to h$, and the bee goes home. Its flight path on this occasion will have started with a right turn of 45° and a straight flight of 20 metres. Then it will have found food, turned left through 90°, flown 1 metre and failed to find food. This goes on until there have been 50 finds, or 150 failures – $\{37 \text{ if } \Sigma F \geqslant 150 \ldots\}$ in rule 31 – when the bee returns to its home base.

Westman's work is a specific example of a systemic analysis of behaviour. We now need to look at general systems theory itself to find out just what a 'system' is and how it differs from something which is not a system. Put simply, a system is an assembly of component parts connected in an organized way. It is singled out by someone for a particular purpose, and what is treated as 'the system' on one occasion may be a mere component, or the environment within which a smaller system operates, on another occasion. The system is not a natural unit but is *defined* as a system in its own right once somebody has decided to treat it as such for the purposes of analysis or design. Its line of demarcation from the outside world, its 'boundary', is something which depends on the definition of the system but nevertheless plays an important part in understanding its properties. Another defining property of a system is the intimate nature of the interconnections between its parts, which typically interact to such a degree that they lose their properties once they are removed from the system, and the system itself may cease to function. Because of this characteristic of systems, it is important to understand the function of the parts while they are *still in the system*, and this poses a grave methodological problem, since most experimental techniques work by separating things out, so as to study them in isolation. What is often needed is a *holistic* technique which will allow the *complete system* to be studied.

Systems show dynamic behaviour: they do things, and they change as a result of interacting forces and processes. They can sometimes be isolated from the rest of the world, neither affecting nor responding to it, in which case they are called closed systems; or they can interact with an environment outside their boundary, in which case they are called open systems. Most complex systems are capable of achieving and maintaining an equilibrium. Whether they are social, economic or biological systems, they tend towards certain states by means of a regularized pattern of exchanges of energy, material or information within the system, and in the case of open systems, with their environment. Systems have inbuilt mechanisms which make them self-regulating and self-maintaining. One interesting property of many systems is their capacity to resist change in a changing environment, as well as to produce change. This is the capacity of *homeostasis*, meaning 'staying the same'. Think, for instance, of an automatic pilot which holds an aircraft on course regardless of variations in wind, turbulence or cloud density, by constantly monitoring and cancelling discrepancies between the desired and the actual course, using the process called negative feedback.

Systems can also be either 'discrete' or 'continuous'. A continuous system deals with variables such as pressure, on a sliding scale without separate steps or states. In discrete systems, on the other hand, the components can only be in one of a number of distinct states, like a digital computer which switches from state to state as it calculates. Systems can be further divided into probabilistic and deterministic types. A deterministic system is one that follows a fixed course of events and can be predicted with absolute certainty, at least in principle. A probabilistic system is less predictable. Its next state is not *determined* by previous states and circumstances, but the *probability* of each possibility materializing as the next state changes with previous states and circumstances.

## Cybernetics: the steersmanship of complex systems

Another discipline which plays a part in our understanding of complex systems is cybernetics. The name 'cybernetics' comes from the Greek word meaning 'steersmanship' or 'helmsmanship', which is rather apt when applied to self-regulating systems. Today the discipline is usually defined as the 'science of communication and control' and is more or less synonymous with control engineering and its application to the study of natural systems, where control mechanisms such as negative-feedback loops are often found maintaining steady states in the face of change.

## Sudden change and catastrophe

Catastrophe theory is a branch of applied topology (the mathematical study of shapes) which has been used to highlight interesting and otherwise enigmatic properties of certain behavioural systems. Earlier we mentioned the difference between discrete and continuous systems. Each is fairly straightforward to deal with individually, but problems arise when a system contains a combination of discrete and continuous elements. In a certain class of systems, the variables to which they respond (the input variables) are continuous, but the outputs are discrete, over either the whole range or part of the range of responses. Consider the example of driving an increasing number of lorries over a rather fragile bridge. This is a mechanical system whose input variable is the load on the bridge at any given moment. The output variable of the system is the amount of strain or deformation which is induced in the structure of the bridge. The relation between input and output could be represented by a simple equation or function, showing the relation between increasing load and increased strain. This is fine until the bridge exceeds its maximum load and collapses – a situation that is highly relevant and should not be left out of the account, but that cannot be easily accommodated in the picture of continuous, reversible, corresponding change in deformation with load. A sudden and dramatic 'discrete' change has been brought about by a small change in a continuous input variable, and this is known as a 'catastrophe' or more generally, a singularity. (Even if the event is not disastrous, it is still called a catastrophic change, because a sudden discrete change of state has interrupted a previously continuous output.)

Although the example of the bridge provides a simple illustration of the point, it is the application of catastrophe theory to human behaviour which is of greater interest here. It has been suggested that human aggression might be thought of in this way. The amount of provocation a person is exposed to combines with the severity of the conflict to produce a particular level of anger, as shown by the rather curious folded catastrophe surface in Figure 46. The more provocation people experience, the more angry they will become; and as the provocation dies away they will become less angry. We might expect an individual's level of arousal to be driven up or down as a continuous function, depending on the increasing or decreasing level of provocation from others. But what happens if the conflict is long

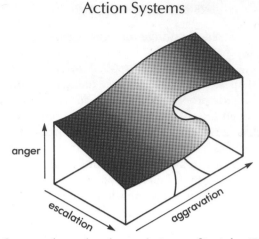

*Figure 46*   Catastrophe surface for escalating conflict (after Zeeman 1976)

drawn out and acrimonious? The reactions could escalate and take on a new character, with different relationships between anger and provocation. On the three-dimensional catastrophe plot, the back edge of the upper 'behaviour' surface shows the simple curvilinear relationship between provocation and anger, rising and falling together. The third dimension, which comes towards you out of the page, represents escalation. As the argument becomes more and more acrimonious and protracted, the parts of the surface nearer the front become involved; here the surface develops a 'fold', which represents the nature and properties of the catastrophe to which this system is prone. The middle layer of the fold can be discounted as a 'quasi-surface' or unstable region. It represents sets of conditions which would immediately change to reach some other more stable state. On the front regions of the surface, below the fold, the anger level can only increase smoothly until it reaches the point where the surface folds back into an unstable region, and then it will suddenly jump up to a different and higher level. There is no way back down to the lower continuous slope until the left-hand edge of the unstable region is reached. This is called the downward catastrophe, where the individual's anger level drops from the lip, back on to the lower surface, and the former state of affairs is restored.

In general, there are five distinguishing properties of catastrophic systems, called bimodality, discontinuity, hysteresis, inaccessible regions and divergence. We shall go through each of these characteristics in turn, to see how catastrophic systems in general behave.

First, bimodality refers to the two separate modes of behaviour between which the system 'flips', shown in Figure 46 as the two stable layers of the behaviour surface. There can be no gradual change from one to the other, only a sudden jump. This is the meaning of discontinuity. Hysteresis, the third feature, is a property which is also found in physical systems. For example, if a magnetic field is applied to a piece of iron, and the extent of its magnetization is measured as the field increases, a magnetization curve is built up. If the metal is *de*-magnetized by reversing the field, the metal does not lose its magnetism by retracing the same pathway. Instead, it follows a different curve back to its initial state, so that over all a loop, called a hysteresis loop, is formed on the graph of magnetization and demagnetization. In general hysteresis is the property by which a process runs forwards and backwards along different trajectories. This is what happens in a catastrophic system. The points at which the upward and downward catastrophes occur are different, so a hysteresis loop is set up as the system goes through a cycle of upward and downward catastrophes. The fourth property of a catastrophic system is the inaccessible or unstable nature of certain combinations of conditions which make up part of the behaviour surface. Fifthly, there is the interesting property known as divergence. Starting on the centre rear part of the behaviour surface, two trajectories coming forward – two courses of events produced by nearly identical circumstances – could result in vastly different outcomes, on the upper and lower folds of the surface. Rather remarkably the differences between the two sets of circumstances can tend to zero, without any reduction in the difference of outcomes.

The relevance of catastrophe theory for our purpose here is that many action systems are catastrophic, that is they are liable to respond to continuous changes in circumstance with discrete changes in behaviour. Most techniques of systems modelling can only cope if the system to be represented is entirely continuous or entirely discrete, and, since that is often not so, the ability of catastrophe theory to deal with the 'hybrid' cases makes it a specially useful tool.

## Automata: imaginary computers

We shall look next at a very different mathematical formulation used to describe complex sequences of events over time, known as 'automata theory'. This theory has historical links with generative grammar, to which it contributed among other things a taxonomy of possible classes of grammars.

Try to solve the following problem. You have to design a system that can function like a computer or a brain. It must be capable of taking in a variety of symbols through its input channels, and then returning various other symbols through its output channels to the world. You must conceive of an overall design that will allow it to carry out any form of calculation, and a notation that will encapsulate all the different rules and regularities which might govern the system. These rules must be clearly and rigorously defined, and their different formats must relate in a theoretically useful manner to the level of complexity or power of the overall system. Such a problem and its classical solution were devised by Alan Turing, a mathematician interested in the limits of computability. Turing wanted to determine which mathematical problems were soluble in principle, and which were not, even using forms of mathematics not yet invented. To do this it was necessary to find and state the limits of all possible calculations. For this he invented and characterized an (imaginary) computer, called a Turing machine. It is a 'universal machine' in that its capabilities are provably coextensive with the domain of all possible stepwise determinate reasoning procedures. *Inter alia* this has also served as a theoretical framework for the design of real computers, and has provided us with a theoretical language for describing the operations that information-processing systems, including brains, carry out. A Turing machine consists of an infinitely long paper tape, divided into squares, on which the symbols 0 and 1 may be written, and a read and write head which can read the symbols, write new symbols on the tape, and move the tape to the left or right. The power and universality of the machine arises because it need only contain a simple subsystem for interpreting and responding to symbols on the tape. This is its 'finite-state component', shown in Figure 47. Do not worry about the details of this diagram. Its purpose here is only to give an impression of the nature and relative simplicity of the subsystem involved.

All other instructions for a particular calculation could be carried in the symbols on the tape, as they were to be in the program of the later programmable computers. Hence the powers of the machine were as great as the range of possible instructions its tape could give it – but even then were not boundless. This is just the point of interest

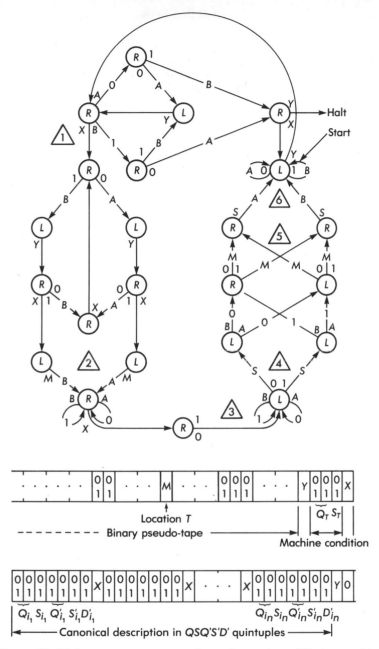

*Figure 47* Finite-state component and tape for a universal Turing machine (from Minsky 1972)

to mathematicians. The Turing machine, or 'Turing automaton', is the most powerful of a family of similar automata, and it is the one which corresponds to the transformational grammar invented by linguists, also known as the 'type-zero grammar', since it is formed by adding no restrictions to the universal specification.

| Automaton | Language | Grammar |
|-----------|----------|---------|
| Finite state | Regular | 3 |
| Pushdown stack | Context-free | 2 |
| Linear-bounded | Context-sensitive | 1 |
| Turing | Transformational | 0 |

*Figure 48*   Classes of automata, languages and grammars

Type-zero grammar is the most complex and powerful, and it can produce and parse extremely complicated strings. Simpler versions can be produced by adding additional constraints or restrictions in its operation. The addition of one, two or three constraints gives rise to a grammar of type one, two or three respectively, each being less powerful than the one before, and carrying out a perfect subset of its possible operations.

Working up the scheme, the next type is the type-one grammar, or linear-bounded automaton, which is, as its name suggests, a Turing-type tape machine with the added restriction that, in reading the symbols on the tape and relating one to another, it is able to operate only within a 'linear bound' or restricted range. It can operate only on a context of finite length when relating symbols to one another, and if any two symbols are further apart than that, they are unrelatable in a machine of this class. This type of automaton or grammar is capable of producing a so-called context-sensitive language, which does not mean that the utterances or the remarks themselves are context-sensitive, which we assume they always would be, but that the rewrite rules underlying the output are context-sensitive. Instead of having a rule like *S rewrites to NP + VP* we could have something like this: *XSY* (meaning S only when in the context of X and Y) *rewrites to NP + VP in the context of X and Y*, or *XSY rewrites to X+NP+VP+Y*. That is a rather more powerful formulation than a context-free rewrite rule because it allows S to be rewritten to different things in different contexts, and thus makes the grammar work more flexibly.

It follows that the next most simple language type has to be the 'context-free language', produced by a type-two grammar. This can follow simple rewrite rules, without reference to the rest of the string in question. The corresponding automaton is known as a 'push-down' stack device, because the operations are stored in a special memory from which the last item stored is the first to be retrieved, just as in the spring-loaded stacks of trays in a cafeteria, from which the metaphor and the name comes.

In Figure 49 the four types of grammar are tabulated, together with a number of formal questions which can be posed about each grammar type. For each combination of a grammar type and a question, the table shows whether the answer is decidable (D), undecidable (U), not yet known (?) or true in all cases (T). For example, the question 'Is the language common to two grammars empty?' is answerable for type three, and undecidable (no algorithm exists for its resolution) with the remaining types. Likewise, 'Is the language generated by a grammar equal to all strings of terminal characters?' or, to put it another way, 'Are all combinations of symbols possible?' is again decidable for type three and undecidable for the other more complex grammar types two, one and zero. These questions show how the rigorous formal specifications of a language or other language-like systems (such as an organized family of possible progressions of events) can be used to infer further properties of the system, and the limits of the range of issues which are formally decidable from the system specification alone. Needless to say this is the kind of theoretical specification, with rigorously deducible consequences, on which the natural sciences have thrived, and which the behavioural sciences have often lacked.

The power and elegance of the machine metaphor can be illustrated in much more detail using the simplest of the family of automata, the finite-state automaton. As with any automaton (or other information-processing system), its primary feature is its capacity to respond systematically to its inputs. The information which comes out is systematically related to the information which goes in. We want an economical but powerful method to describe the possible relationships between the ingoing and outcoming information. This relation is sometimes called the 'transfer function' of the system, since it describes the transfer of information between the input and output. In algebraic terms this relationship can be represented in the following way. The response of the system at time $t + 1$ is some function of its history up until time $t$, and the present

## Decision problems of various grammars

D indicates that there exists an algorithm for deciding this question for this class of grammars.

U indicates that no algorithm exists for deciding this question for this class of grammars.

T indicates that this question is true for all grammars in this class.

? indicates that we do not yet know about the existence or non-existence of an algorithm for deciding this question for this class of grammars.

Following each question, and included in parentheses, is the formal representation of the question. Note that if the question involves two grammars, they are of the same type.

| Question | Class of grammars | | | |
| --- | --- | --- | --- | --- |
| | Type 3 | Type 2 | Type 1 | Type 0 |
| Is the language generated by a grammar empty? $(L_G = 0)$ | D | D | U | U |
| Is the language generated by a grammar infinite? $(L_G$ infinite$)$ | D | D | U | U |
| Is the language generated by a grammar equal to all strings of terminal characters? $(L_G = V_T^*)$ | D | U | U | U |
| Do two grammars generate the same language? $(L_{G_1} = L_{G_2})$ | D | U | U | U |
| For two grammars, is the language of one included in the language of the other? $(L_{G_1} \subseteq L_{G_2})$ | D | U | U | U |
| Is the language common to two grammars empty? $(L_{G_1} \cap L_{G_2} = 0)$ | D | U | U | U |
| Is the language common to two grammars the same type as the grammars? $(L_{G_1} \cap L_{G_2}$ language of same type$)$ | T | U | T | T |
| Is the complement of the language generated by a grammar the same type as the grammar? $(V_T^* - L_G$ language of same type$)$ | T | U | ? | U |
| For any strings $\phi$, $\psi$, can $\psi$ be derived from $\phi$ in a grammar? $(\phi \Rightarrow \psi)$ | D | D | D | U |
| For any strings $\phi$, $\psi$, can some string including $\psi$ be derived from $\phi$ in a grammar? $(\phi \overset{*}{\Rightarrow} \psi)$ | D | D | U | U |
| Is there a sentence in the language of a grammar that can be derived in more than one way in the grammar? $(G$ ambiguous$)$ | D | U | U | U |
| For a grammar, does there exist an unambiguous grammar of the same type that generates the same language? | T | ? | ? | T |

*Figure 49* Decidable and undecidable questions for four classes of grammar (from Meetham 1969)

input or stimulus at time $t$. That is, $R_{t+1} = f(H_t, S_t)$. There is, however, a problem inherent in the term $H_t$, the history up until time $t$, because there is no way of formalizing the entire range of possible histories of inputs in a system like this, since they are both infinitely numerous and indefinitely long. Although the basic equation presents us with this problem, it also holds the seeds of the solution. There is a very neat 'trick' to get around the difficulty. The device we are trying to characterize does not have an infinite capacity for differentiating between various states of affairs in the world, since it has a finite number of states its own mechanism can be in. Consequently, there are a limited number of things between which it can discriminate by creating an internal representation of each, so as to respond to them differently. If there are more possible histories than states of the machine, it would be unable to distinguish them all. For each state there would be a number of different histories which would put the machine into that state, but because the state is the *same* for each of these histories, and is the only representation of them to affect the future behaviour of the machine, no further distinction between them could be made by the machine, or need be made by us.

Now it could be argued that we do not know enough about most interesting systems to know how many states they can have, or what those states would be. Here the argument can be turned on its head. Let us say that, for all practical purposes, each set of histories within which variations make no difference to the future behaviour of the system is a state. In this way we can have all the analytical power of an internal view of the state structure of the machine, but on the basis of external criteria alone. For a simple pocket calculator, for instance, one may not know how many states of its circuitry there could be, but a number of things about its states are clear. Entering $1 + 2 + 3$ puts it in the same state as entering $3 + 2 + 1$. Any sequence of key presses ending in CLEAR produces the same state. The sequences $+0$, $-0$, $\times 1$, $\div 1$ do not produce a change of state, and so on. The simple message is this. The working of any information-processing system can be studied in terms of its states and their connections, and the states can be determined from the outside, in so far as sets of histories with identical implications for the future can be detected. This idea lends itself to far more sophisticated conceptions of sequential regularity, and the processes producing it, than any we saw in the previous chapter.

Having exploited the limited capacity of the machine for distinguishing between sequences of inputs and for creating different internal representations in response to them, we now need to define the relationship between input(s) and the resulting states. We can propose two tractable functions which specify the system. First, the system's response at time $t + 1$ is now a function *not* of its history, but rather of its present *state* and the present input. This relation is given by $f$, the 'next-response function'. (The letter Q is used to represent the machine's internal state, and $Q_t$ is the machine's state at time $t$.) Finally, we need a means of describing the system's changes from state to state. This is done by the 'next-state function' $g$. It shows what the next state of the machine will be with the expression $Q_{t+1} = g (Q_t, S_t)$. With these two types of function one can completely specify any finite-state automaton.

$$R_{t+1} = f(H_t, S_t)$$
$$\overline{\phantom{R_{t+1} = f(H_t, S_t)}}$$
$$R_{t+1} = f(Q_t, S_t)$$
$$Q_{t+1} = g(Q_t, S_t)$$

*Figure 50*   Next-response and next-state functions for finite-state automata (from Minsky 1972)

So far our description of finite-state automata has been rather abstract, so now we shall go through a couple of simple examples of such an automaton in operation. More elaborate examples may be found in the work of John Chandler, a barrister by training and currently an industrialist. Chandler carried out a cybernetic analysis of the First World War. He used a finite-state system to explicate a number of alternative courses of events and their underlying constraints and regularities. Our examples will just deal with simple arithmetic manipulations, but the principles are much the same.

Let us consider a simple machine that has two states called X and Y, two inputs called 0 and 1, and two outputs also called 0 and 1. Figure 51 shows the next-state function $(g)$ and next-response function $(f)$ for two simple devices. Each table shows the resulting changes for any possible combination of present state and input. So for present state X or Y, and present input 0 or 1, we can find out what the subsequent machine state would be, and from the lower tables giving function $f$, what the systems' next response would be for each combination of state and input. Although this information can be represented as two functions, as shown in the upper part of

| g | X | Y |
|---|---|---|
| 0 | X | X |
| 1 | Y | Y |

| g | X | Y |
|---|---|---|
| 0 | Y | Y |
| 1 | X | X |

| f | X | Y |
|---|---|---|
| 0 | 0 | 1 |
| 1 | 0 | 1 |

| f | X | Y |
|---|---|---|
| 0 | 0 | 1 |
| 1 | 0 | 1 |

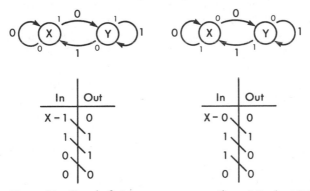

State space diagrams

*Figure 51* Simple finite-state automata (from Minsky 1972)

Figure 51, it can also be translated into 'state-space notation' which is easier to interpret. This is the same notation that was used earlier in the Turing machine diagram in Figure 47. Different points in the space represent different states, hence the name state-space notation. This makes it very easy to read off the appropriate outputs and next state, given a particular state and input. With this useful tool the entire architecture of any system of this type can be mapped, no matter how complex it is.

The arrows linking states show which state the machine would go to next, from the state at the tail of the arrow, given the input on the tail of the arrow. In the process it would give the output shown on the body of the arrow. Put yet another way, each specifying rule or feature of the system can be captured with four pieces of information, for which reason they are called quadruples. The quadruple X, O, X, O, giving a state, input, next state and next response, in that order, captures all the information in the top left-hand cells of the first machine's $g$ and $f$ functions, or the extreme left-hand arrow of its state-space diagram. The first machine is completely specified by the four quadruples X, O, X, O; X, 1, Y, O; Y, O, X, 1; and Y, 1, Y, 1.

What, then, are the system's overall properties? The first of these two devices could be described as a 'one-step memory machine'. In other words it is a machine which, regardless of what state it is in, and what string of inputs it receives, will store every character for one time unit, and then output it again. For example, if the system starts from state X with an input of 1, the state-space diagram shows that O is the next output and the next state of the machine is Y. Then, regardless of the next input, it will output a 1. It does not matter where the machine starts on the map, what state it is in, or what input signals are supplied; its constant property will *always* be that one time unit later whatever has been input will come out. The second machine, on the right-hand side of Figure 51, does the converse, and outputs the opposite signal after a delay of one time unit.

Simpleminded though this may seem, a few elaborations to these basic 'circuits' will produce arithmetic machines that can add, subtract, multiply or divide any pair of numbers, interconvert serial and parallel signals, and so on. This is not far from the design of a basic calculating device, and its great advantage is that it is all in the abstract. This is a 'software' circuit showing the interdependency of information states. The *realization* of this logical design could be in anything from silicon chips to water jets, and yet the calculational principles would remain the same.

Having met the idea that a finite-state device of any complexity is completely specified by a set of quadruples, a listing of the next output and state for each possible combination of input and state, we are now much better able to understand the full power and elegance of the Turing machine itself. Any specific Turing-type machine can be specified with a set of quintuples, five-item groups giving the next state, next tape position, and next item to be written on the tape, for each possible combination of present state and present input (the symbol to be read at the present tape position). All a *universal* Turing machine need consist of then is a piece of finite-state apparatus which can read and act upon a tape which carries on one particular section the list of quintuples specifying the particular characteristics the machine is to have on that occasion. As we saw from Figure 47, this turns out to be surprisingly simple. There is a more general point here too. Turing machines, real computers and arguably brains are universal 'machines' in that they contain enough basic structure to act upon the particular specifications of an infinite set of *particular* machines, in such a way as to simulate or mimic the characteristics of each particular machine. In that sense, running a program in a computer is like simulating a special-purpose circuit with particular properties and functions, within a general-purpose circuit. So in a way the machine, despite its potential to be many other things too, *becomes* temporarily the device of which its program is the specification.

Now to liken the relation of mind to brain with the relation of computer software to hardware is only a loose and imperfect analogy, but nevertheless there may be a comparable sense in which our brains develop particular properties out of their more general potentialities under the influence of incoming information, and we become neurophysiologically what our experience dictates. That is not just to say that learning changes us, although it clearly does, but that describing psychological functioning in software rather than hardware terms is more than just a provisional account, which we have to make do with until we can undertake a *biological* description of what is *really* happening in the brain. It may be that the *programs* of the brain (which loosely speaking equal the mind) do provide an autonomous and even primary level of explanation for human conduct, to which comparatively little is added by a knowledge of its physical realization in nerve tissue. It is certainly the case that an understanding of hardware is completely irrelevant to much of what can be understood about a computer from its software. To a remarkable degree, software engineering and hardware engineering have developed into quite separate disciplines in the computer world, with surprisingly little to say to each other. The same future may well be in store for physiological and psychological studies of mind, brain and behaviour. However, this does *not* imply a *metaphysical* dualism in which minds and brains (or programs and circuits) are separate and autonomously (or interactively) functioning mechanisms. They are still one and the same thing.

## Mathematical nerves

Can one extend this kind of theorizing to envisage how networks of nerve cells might function as calculating devices and control systems? Using some stylized hypothetical nerve-cell-like units called McCulloch-Pitts nodes, it is possible to design logic circuits with provable properties, to show *in principle* how nerve tissue *might* carry out its various 'electronic' functions in a way that is comprehensible in engineering terms.

The sort of units needed in a calculating device are such things as 'AND gates', 'OR gates', and so on. These are places where signals meet and interact. For instance, in the case of an 'AND gate', if both of two signals arrive simultaneously a third, output signal is generated. Alternatively, in an 'OR gate', the arrival of either of two signals will trigger the output. The McCulloch-Pitts nodes can reproduce these sorts of properties using only stylized nerve cells. Figure 52 shows three such units. Each circle represents the head of a 'nerve cell', and the 'tails' to the right depict the axon which would convey the outgoing pulse to other nerve cells. The number on each cell is its threshold. Excitatory inputs are shown as arrowheads, while inhibitory inputs are shown as small white blobs. The cell with two inputs and a threshold of 2 is an 'AND gate'. That is, it will fire when both of its inputs fire. The cell with a threshold of 1 is an 'OR gate' and will fire when either of its inputs fires. Many other basic logic elements can be built up in this way, using this notation. One of the more interesting implications of the notation is found in the 'universal cell', the third type shown in Figure 52. This is a single cell type

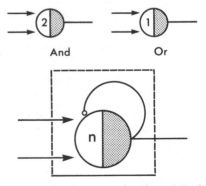

And          Or

*Figure 52*    McCulloch-Pitts nodes (from Minsky 1972)

which could function as a standard unit for a universal calculator. That is, any logic circuit could be built using only this type of cell. This is only possible if the cell is refractory (meaning that once it has fired it cannot fire again immediately). This is notated by splitting the output axon and making part of it an inhibitory input (or negative feedback) to the same cell, although that is not how a real nerve cell comes to be refractory. This is highly abstracted from the laws governing real nerve tissue, but nevertheless it does raise the rather interesting question: why is real nerve tissue refractory? What function does this characteristic serve? The obvious answer is that refractoriness is not functional at all but is merely an inevitable by-product of the cells' need to 'rest and recover' after activity.

The McCulloch-Pitts analysis, on the other hand, raises the *possibility* that the refractoriness of real nerve tissue *is* functional, and is a necessary property by virtue of which nerve cells can function as universal electronic units, from which any type of 'circuit' could be built.

## Grammatical machines

We have considered grammars as analogues for action, and automata as analogues for action. The next step is to combine the two, and consider automata which can process grammatical structures.

The particular linguistic parsing automaton shown in Figure 53

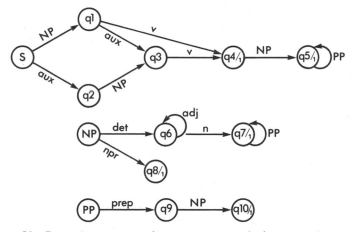

*Figure 53*     Recursive augmented transition network (from Woods 1970)

has overall design principles as powerful as a Turing machine, but there are some differences in notation and format which entitle it to a different name. This system is called a recursive augmented transition network, or RATN for short. Figure 53 shows an RATN looking rather like a state-space diagram. Again there are nodes representing states, and transitions shown as arrows pointing to new states. But this is an unusual network, which can jump from one part, on which it is currently working, to use that whole segment again as a test for one of its own subcomponents, which is why it is called recursive. The network is termed 'augmented' because, as it goes from one state to the next, it leaves a trace showing the overall structure of the sentence it has found. This notation allows one to design programs which will parse and identify well-formed structures in natural language. The networks are capable of recognizing a correct and grammatical sentence, or rejecting incorrect sentences. The numbers in the state circles are state labels. Those which have a '/1' next to them are possible terminating states. If the network is in one of these states when it runs out of sentence, that means it has reached a legitimate ending-point, and the sentence is well formed. If it runs out of sentence when it is in one of the other states, that means the sentence is incomplete. The fragment shown in Figure 53 can recognize both the structure and the well-formedness of sentences like 'Did the red barn collapse?' or 'John washed the car', and can also reject as ill-formed such constructions as 'Did she bring the yellow. . . ?'

Let us see briefly how that works. The network starts off in state S. To go from that state into the next, it has to satisfy one or other of the conditions *noun phrase found next* or *auxiliary found next*. What it finds in the first example is 'Did', the auxiliary verb, and so it goes into state 2. To leave state 2 it must find a noun phrase, which it does, namely 'the red barn'. This would take it to state 3. However, since there are quite a number of words involved in detecting the noun phrase, it cannot just make the test 'by inspection' – it is not merely a question of looking at a single word and identifying its type. It is a rather more complicated business to satisfy the noun-phrase condition and thus move from state 2 to state 3. In order to do this, the main network is put on 'hold' for the time being, in the state it is in, while the system jumps to a different piece of network, shown lower down in Figure 53, which embodies the test for a noun phrase. Here the system functions just as in the main network. To detect a noun phrase, the conditions *pronoun* or *determiner* must be satisfied. In this case the condition *determiner* is satisfied by 'the', the definite article in the phrase 'the red barn'. The system is now in state 6. From there it has to find either a noun or an adjective, and it finds another adjective, 'red', putting it back into state 6 again, and then a noun, 'barn', taking it to 7/1, where that segment ends. The system can now jump back to 3, and then find 'collapse', which meets the *verb* condition, and so move to 4/1, which is a successful termination for that particular parsing. In much the same way there are a good many other simple assertions and questions which this network will parse. If you think of some ill-formed word strings, you will be able to see, by following through Figure 53, how the network detects and rejects these.

## Practical systems

Having dealt with abstract principles, we shall now consider some concrete illustrations. The first example comes from a study done by John Breaux when he was at the Surrey University Fire Research Unit. The task was to develop a single coherent account of physical and behavioural processes in burning buildings. A mathematical model was available, describing the rate at which smoke, flame and melting materials accumulated and spread through the building, and there was also behavioural information about survivors and casualties from eyewitnesses, coroners' reports, and post-mortems. These seemingly irreconcilable descriptions of the problem dealt particularly with fires in multiple-occupancy buildings, such as hotels and hospitals, where casualties in fires are often surprisingly high. Using techniques like those described in Chapter 3, the behavioural data were reduced to flow diagrams, rather like state-space diagrams. A simple example can be seen in Figure 54 in the decomposition diagram for behaviour in multiple-occupancy buildings on fire. The figure shows the behavioural states that were involved and their interconnections.

   This is, however, only a simple account. The overall pattern described by Breaux was rather more complicated. Networks were drawn showing the distinctive choices of the survivors, and of the casualties and fatalities. It was important to pinpoint the essence of the difference between those people who successfully escaped from the burning buildings, and those who did not, but to do this it seemed

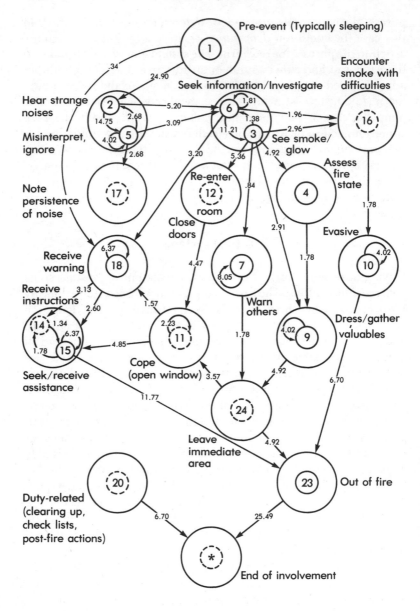

*Figure 54* Decomposition diagram for behaviour in multiple-occupancy buildings on fire (from Canter, Breaux and Sime 1978)

that a real-time description of the behaviour was necessary, whereas all that was available was a series of narratives. These narratives were rescaled on the basis of the likely duration of each event, to provide a time axis for the reports. It was also discovered that the sequences of events in the narratives could be overlapped and matched, so as to reconstruct a single overall series. Methods devised by Coombs were used to measure the extent to which each fragment of behaviour was or was not legitimately describable as a segment from one larger overall sequence. In this case the narratives could be approximated to a single overall sequence, which then formed the basis of the reconstructed time dimension.

Breaux next examined the diversity of attempts to leave the building at each stage of the fire, for the two populations – the survivors and the non-survivors. Both non-survivors and survivors started off by doing the same sort of things. As the fires often occurred at night, it was quite typical for everyone to be asleep in bed at the outset. Likewise towards the end of the sequence there was little behavioural variety within the two populations. It was the *central* time period which was of particular interest, because here people were engaged in a wide range of behaviours. It was found that the growth and decay of diversity takes a very different time course for the individuals who survive and for those who die in the fire. For survivors there is a sudden increase in the diversity of the behavioural sequence early on, while the victims exhibit a smaller and more protracted pattern of behavioural variation. As Figure 55 shows, those who stay alive react quickly to the incidence of fire, and

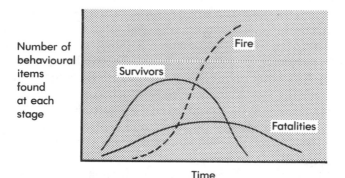

*Figure 55*   Behavioural profiles of survivors and those who die in building fires (after J. Breaux)

respond with vigorous and varied attempts to escape, whereas those who die tend to react more slowly. By superimposing the 'fire-growth function' – the rate at which flames and smoke spread throughout the building – on the behavioural curves of the two populations, a disturbing graphic representation of the problem can be revealed. The first behavioural-diversity peak occurs *before* the fire begins to engulf the building. Those individuals will escape. The remaining individuals are swept along by the advancing flame and smoke fronts, which encroach more and more on their possible effective escape routes, and these are the people who will die in the fire.

Much of the variance between fast and slow responders, with their subsequently different chances of survival, is accounted for in the case of hotels by the size of the party the people are staying with. Members of families and other groups tend to look for the others, and delay their own escape, especially when the others have already escaped and so for that reason cannot be found. The danger of death or injury in hotel fires is far greater for members of a party than for individual guests. These and other more detailed findings are now available for use in the design of buildings, the reassessment of hotel policies for the allocation of rooms, and new legislation. Abstract and sometimes highly technical analyses of action systems do have real practical consequences.

## The world as an action system

One final example of behaviour systems analysis will round off this chapter, and the book as a whole. This particular model represents an extremely large and important system to all of us, namely the whole world and its future. Figure 56 shows one of Forrester's 'systems dynamics' models of the world. The model represents the interplay between economic, ecological and behavioural variables throughout the world. It incorporates such correlations as exist between for example food production, birth rate, death rate, capital investment, environmental pollution, and depletion of natural resources. Models of this sort are now often criticized for being over-aggregated. That is, there is only one pool of factors to depict the entire world, with no attempt to differentiate between the properties and problems of widely different regions such as India and North America. Everybody and every country is combined into one simple set of variables covering populations, capital investment, natural resources, quality of life, and so on. As with Figure 47, the details do not matter here so much as a general impression of the extent and complexity of the network of interacting subcomponents.

Forrester makes the rather attractive claim that common sense can define the important variables, and the individual relationships between them. It seems obvious that, if industrial investment increases, then so does pollution, or that more people would mean that more food would be needed. The basic relations between elements in the influence diagram are not usually a matter for empirical study. They should be self-evident. What is far from obvious is how we infer and manipulate the consequences of all these relations and processes acting in concert. That is precisely the difficulty the model is designed to overcome. When implemented as a computer simulation, the model can be supplied with different sets of conditions and alternative policies so that (tentative) predictions of their future consequences can be made.

Figure 57 shows the projection for one particular set of conditions and policies up to the year 2100. The early parts of the curve from 1900 until the 1960s were used to estimate parameters for the model, so that it could reproduce the known course of events to date. It is not enough to know that certain things increase with certain other things, unless you know specifically what coefficients and exponents to use in the equations describing the specific relations involved. The remainder of the curves, to the right of Figure 57, show a projection for the simplest case with policies allowed to remain roughly as they are now. The worrying result is that the quality of life declines very rapidly. Natural resources decline first, and it is this which drives the general deterioration of everything else, in this particular case. The population increases and then declines, because it is no longer possible to feed and house the increased number of people. Capital investment declines, pollution peaks, and then that too goes down again, because of declining industrial production. All in all, things start to look very bleak indeed. By about the year 2050 the crunch really comes, if policies are left as they are. But of course, in the model one can easily change the policies to see what happens, and this is the whole point of such a model. We can try having less capital investment, or strict birth-control laws, or turning all our resources over to agricultural production, or a variety of other things. In each case different curves and different projections result, but nevertheless

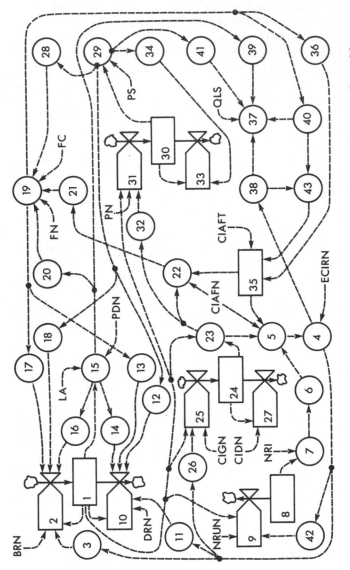

Levels are represented by rectangles; rates by valves; auxiliaries (significant components of rates) by circles; dotted lines indicate directions, shown by arrows.

**Key**

1 Population
2 Birth rate
3 Birth rate from material multiplier
4 Material standard of living
5 Effective capital investment ratio
6 Natural resources extraction multiplier
7 Natural resources—fraction remaining
8 Natural resources
9 Natural resources—usage rate
10 Death rate
11 Death rate from material multiplier
12 Death rate from pollution multiplier
13 Death rate from food multiplier
14 Death rate from crowding multiplier
15 Crowding ratio
16 Birth rate from crowding multiplier
17 Birth rate from food multiplier
18 Birth rate from pollution multiplier
19 Food ratio
20 Food from crowding multiplier
21 Food potential from capital investment
22 Capital investment ratio in agriculture
23 Capital investment ratio
24 Capital investment
25 Capital investment generation
26 Capital investment multiplier
27 Capital investment discard
28 Food from pollution multiplier
29 Pollution ratio
30 Pollution

31 Pollution generation
32 Pollution from capital multiplier
33 Pollution absorption
34 Pollution absorption time
35 Capital investment in agriculture—fraction
36 Capital fraction indicated by food ratio
37 Quality of life
38 Quality of life from material
39 Quality of life from crowding
40 Quality of life from food
41 Quality of life from pollution
42 Natural resources from material multiplier
43 Capital investment from quality ratio

BRN    Birth rate normal
CIAFN  Capital investment in agriculture fraction normal
CIAFT  Capital investment in agriculture fraction adjustment time
CIDN   Capital investment discard normal
CIGN   Capital investment generation normal
DRN    Death rate normal
ECIRN  Effective capital investment ratio normal
FC     Food coefficient
FN     Food normal
LA     Land area
NRI    Natural resources initial
NRUN   Natural resources usage normal
PDN    Population density normal
PN     Pollution normal
PS     Pollution standard
QLS    Quality of life standard

*Figure 56*   Flow diagram of the world (from Forrester 1972)

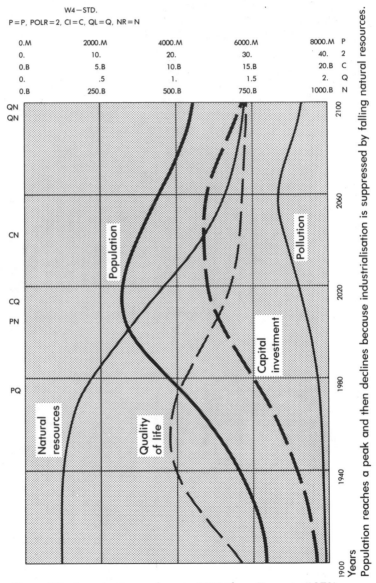

*Figure 57* A projection to the year 2100 (from Forrester 1972)

they all seem to involve a major upheaval in about the year 2050, but for quite different reasons. It appears at first from this model that our option is not whether to face disaster in about 2050, but only the means by which we come to precipitate it. It can be driven by pollution, starvation, overpopulation, or depletion of natural resources, depending on the policy we choose, but it is not easy to avert the disaster altogether. Whatever makes one problem better makes another one worse.

However, we do not want to end on a gloomy note. Things are probably not as bad as they seemed at first. This was a very early model, and a rather naïve one at that, in some ways. Since then people have produced much more elaborate models. They have taken account of more varied policy options, and of the differences between different national sectors. They have put more information and more thought into the models, and happily the news is that, as the models get better, the predictions also become more hopeful again. It looks as though we might avert disaster after all.

But the world is still a dangerous place. All kinds of problems and dilemmas arise, many of them as a result of patterns of human action too complex for us to foresee or allow for adequately. If we could foresee the properties of complex action systems better, if we could exercise more understanding and foresight in trying to manage them, the outlook for the future would be much more hopeful still. The development of new tools, new ideas and new concepts must continue. We must understand the human world as thoroughly as we have come to understand the physical world. The methods will not come from the orthodox behavioural sciences alone, but from all kinds of disciplines with different viewpoints working together. This will involve us all in turning away from our preoccupation with the minutiae of *behaviour*, to look at the more global, abstract and generally familiar units of *action*. Systemic methods – in which complex configurations of entities and processes are studied in their entirety, and not just a piece at a time – will be at a premium. If the results are to be as credible and as useful as they should be, they will have to be built on the commonsense foundations of existing practical activities in much the way that the natural sciences have always been, and the behavioural sciences have seldom even tried to be. This in turn will require us to look at the mainsprings of everyday decision and action which lie outside, but adjacent to, our reportable conscious reasoning faculties – the highest levels in the psychological hierarchy of action control, where emotionally mediated processes lay down the long-term life patterns and strategies which cognitive centres serve to monitor and implement in the shorter-term course of our specific dealings with objects and events in the outside world. In carrying out this programme of research, four procedural problems will have to be overcome: the integration of numerous measures into manageable summaries; the combination of hermeneutic, causal and structural ideas within broader and more coherent explanatory frameworks than we have at present; the codification and prediction of complex patterns of events, extending well into the future; and the systematic representation, evaluation and management of alternative policy options, using systems models to predict the consequences of each decision.

Over all, the unifying theme of this book has been the study of natural action in all its complexity, and in the full richness of the systems which it forms. We hope in future that people will take a fresh look at the perennial problems we face, not just from their own standpoint as psychologists, linguists, engineers or computer scientists, but from the more eclectic perspective in which all these disciplines and more have their part to play, in the unravelling of what we have called *action systems*.

## Further reading

Aleksander, I. (1977) *The Human Machine*. St Saphorin, Switzerland: Georgi.

Annett, J. (1969) *Feedback and Human Behaviour*. Harmondsworth: Penguin.

Ashby, R. (1952) *Design for a Brain*. London: Chapman & Hall.

Ashby, R. (1956) *An Introduction to Cybernetics*. London: Chapman & Hall.

Battersby, A. (1975) *Mathematics in Management*. 2nd edn. Harmondsworth: Penguin.

Beishon, J., and Peters, G. (1976) *Systems Behaviour*. London: Harper & Row, for the Open University Press.

Boden, M. (1977) *Artificial Intelligence and Natural Man*. Hassocks: Harvester.

Bossel, H., Klaczko, S., and Müller, N. (eds), (1976) *Systems Theory in the Social Sciences*. Basle: Birkhauser.

Box, G. E. P., and Jenkins, G. M. (1976) *Time Series Analysis, Forecasting and Control*. San Francisco, Cal.: Holden-Day.

Brockman, J., and Rosenfeld, E. (1973) *Real Time: A Catalogue of Ideas and Information*. London: Pan.

Bullock, A., and Stallybrass, O. (eds) (1977) *The Fontana Dictionary of Modern Thought*. London: Fontana.

Canter, D., Breaux, J., and Sime, J. (1978) *Human Behaviour in Fires*. Building Research Establishment, Fire Research Station. Guildford: University of Surrey.

Chandler, W. J. (1979) 'A science of history'. Doctoral thesis, Uxbridge: University of Surrey.

Chomsky, N. (1959) 'On certain formal properties of grammar'. *Information and Control*, 1, 91–112.

Clark, J. A., and Cole, H. S. D. (1975) *Global Simulation Models: A Comparative Study*. Chichester: Wiley.

Cook, N. D. (1980) *Stability and Flexibility: An Analysis of Natural Systems*. Oxford: Pergamon.

Coyle, R. G. (1977) *Management Systems Dynamics*. Chichester: Wiley.

De Greene, K. B. (1980) 'Major conceptual problems in the systems management of human factors/ergonomics research'. *Ergonomics*, 23 (1), 3–11.

Dreyfus, M. L. (1972) *What Computers Can't Do: A Critique of Artificial Reason*. New York: Harper & Row.

Fodor, J. A. (1981) 'The mind–body problem'. *Scientific American*, 244 (1), 124–32.

Forrester, J. W. (1972) 'Understanding the counterintuitive behaviour of social systems'. In J. Beishon and G. Peters (eds), *Systems Behaviour*. London: Harper & Row.

Freeman, C., and Jahoda, M. (eds) (1978) *World Futures: The Great Debate*. Oxford: Robertson.

George, F. (1971) *Teach Yourself Cybernetics*. London: English Universities Press.

Gregory, R. (1961) 'The brain as an engineering problem'. In W. H. Thorpe and O. L. Zangwill (eds), *Current Problems in Animal Behaviour*. Cambridge: Cambridge University Press.

Hirsch, F. (1977) *The Social Limits to Growth*. London: Routledge & Kegan Paul.

Hofstadter, D. R. (1979) *Gödel, Escher, Bach: An Eternal Golden Braid*. Hassocks: Harvester.

Isnard, C. A., and Zeeman, E. C. (1976) 'Some models from catastrophe theory in the social sciences'. In L. Collins (ed.), *The Use of Models in the Social Sciences*. London: Tavistock.

Johnson-Laird, P. N., and Wason, P. C. (eds) (1977) *Thinking: Readings in Cognitive Science*. Cambridge: Cambridge University Press.

Kaufman, A. (1972) *Points and Arrows*. London: Transworld Student Library.

Kaufman, G. M., and Thomas, H. (1977) *Modern Decision Analysis*. Harmondsworth: Penguin.

Knight, D. E., Curtis, H. W., and Fogel, L. J. (eds) (1971) *Cybernetics, Simulation and Conflict Resolution*. New York: Spartan.

Laszlo, E. (1972) *The Systems View of the World*. Oxford: Blackwell.

Lighthill, J. (ed.) (1978) *Newer Uses of Mathematics*. Harmondsworth: Penguin.

Lumsden, C. J., and Wilson, E. O. (1981) *Genes, Mind and Culture: The Coevolutionary Process*. Cambridge, Mass.: Harvard University Press.

McFarland, D. J. (1971) *Feedback Mechanisms in Animal Behaviour*. London: Academic Press.

McFarland, D. J. (ed.) (1974) *Motivational Control Systems Analysis*. London: Academic Press.

Makower, M. S., and Williamson, E. (1967) *Operational Research*. London: English Universities Press.

Marshall, J. C. (1977) 'Minds, machines and metaphors'. *Social Studies of Science*, 7, 475–88.

Meetham, A. R. (1969) *Encyclopaedia of Linguistics Information and Control*. Oxford: Pergamon.

Miller, G. A., and Johnson-Laird, P. N. (1976) *Language and Perception*. Cambridge: Cambridge University Press.

Minsky, M. (1972) *Computation: Finite and Infinite Machines*. London: Prentice-Hall.

Nagel, S. S. (1976) *Operations Research Methods. Quantitative Applications in the Social Sciences*, no. 2. Beverly Hills, Cal.: Sage.

Newbold, P. (1973) *Forecasting Methods. Civil Service College Occasional papers*, 18. London: HMSO.

Newell, A., and Simon, H. (1972) *Human Problem Solving*. Englewood Cliffs, NJ: Prentice-Hall.

Powers, W. T. (1973) *Behaviour: The Control of Perception*. Chicago, Ill.: Aldine.

Schank, R. C. (1973) 'Identification of conceptualizations underlying natural language'. In R. C. Schank and K. M. Colby (eds), *Computer Models of Thought and Language*. San Francisco, Cal.: Freeman.

Schank, R. C., and Abelson, R. P. (1977) *Scripts, Plans, Goals and Understanding*. Hillsdale, NJ: Erlbaum.

Stewart, I. (1975) *Concepts of Modern Mathematics*. Harmondsworth: Penguin.

Stewart, N. I., and Peregoy, P. I. (1983) 'Catastrophe theory modelling in psychology'. *Psychological Bulletin*, 94 (2), 336–62.

Turing, A. M. (1950) 'Computing machinery and intelligence'. *Mind*, 59, 433–60.

Waddington, C. H. (1977) *Tools for Thought (about Complex Systems)*. St Albans: Paladin.

Waddington, C. H. (1978) *The Man-Made Future*. London: Croom-Helm.

Weizenbaum, J. (1976) *Computer Power and Human Reason*. San Francisco, Cal.: Freeman.

Westman, R. S. (1977) 'Environmental languages and the functional bases of animal behaviour'. In B. Hazlett (ed.), *Quantitative Methods in Animal Behaviour*. New York: Academic Press.

Wills, G., with Wilson, R., Manning, N., and Hildebrandt, R. (eds) (1972) *Technological Forecasting*. Harmondsworth: Pelican.

Woods, W. A. (1970) 'Transition network grammars for natural language'. *Communications of the ACM*, 13, 591–606.

Zeeman, E. C. (1976) 'Catastrophe theory'. *Scientific American*, 234 (4), 65–83.

# Index